D1044762

MAGIC ACROSS THE TABLE

Other books on magic, magicians, and magic fun by Bill Severn

MAGIC WHEREVER YOU ARE

MAGIC AND MAGICIANS

SHADOW MAGIC:
the story of Shadow Play

YOU AND YOUR SHADOW

MAGIC WITH PAPER

MAGIC IN YOUR POCKETS

MAGIC SHOWS YOU CAN GIVE

PACKS OF FUN:
101 Unusual Things to Do
with Playing Cards
and to Know About Them

MAGIC COMEDY:
tricks, skits and clowning

MAGIC ACROSS THE TABLE

by Bill Severn

illustrated by Katharine Wood

DAVID McKAY COMPANY, INC.
NEW YORK

MAGIC ACROSS THE TABLE

LIBRARY OF CONGRESS CATALOG CARD NUMBER: 72-79094
MANUFACTURED IN THE UNITED STATES OF AMERICA

INTRODUCTION

You don't have to put on a public show to enjoy doing magic. As thousands of magic hobbyists all over the world have discovered, entertaining just a friend or two with the sort of magic done *across the table* can be as much fun as standing up before an audience to wave a wand and pull a rabbit from a hat.

But to make it really fun for those who watch, the tricks you show should be more entertaining than the standard puzzles with a coin, a handkerchief or a pack of cards that nearly everybody learns to do. The joy in watching magic, whether it is performed on the stage or at the table, is in the way it is presented. Its charm for an audience is not so much in its trickery as in the illusion of make-believe.

Magic done at the table, even though the props are small and the surroundings informal, should create a theatrical surprise by means of the magical story it presents.

When a person goes to the theater or watches a play on television he knows that the costumes and scenery are theatrical trickery, but he *suspends his disbelief* to pretend that what he sees is really happening. Good magic, wherever it is shown, is the kind that makes the watcher pretend along with the performer for a moment. That way, he isn't merely tricked or puzzled; he enjoys being fooled because he has been entertained.

The tricks in this book are based on secrets so simple that even the beginning performer should be able to devote himself more to the presentation than to the mechanics of them. The methods have been simplified to eliminate all difficult sleight of hand. The props required are those that usually can be found around any home. They can be prepared without special tools or intricate construction and are the sort that can be carried in the pockets to show almost anywhere. But as with all magic, you must practice them often to present them well.

In each case, what happens is first described as it would appear to the person watching it, in the form of a magical story or a little play of make-believe. Then the basic secret is given, without any of the details, for a general understanding of how the effect is produced. The needed props are listed, along with directions for fixing them, and finally there are the instructions for doing the trick.

Don't be discouraged if the detailed instructions seem complicated at first. They are meant to be read with the props in hand, so you can try them, step by step, as you read along. If you do that you will see that some things that take a lot of words to explain really are quite easy to do. They have been written from actual performance and where precise details are given they should be followed carefully until the reason for them is thoroughly understood.

After you try them a few times you may find ways of handling things that are easier for you than those given in the directions. As long as the trick works just as well your way, change it to suit whatever is natural for you. Change the plots and the talk that goes with them to suit your personality. The instructions here should be considered only as suggestions. Part of the fun is changing tricks around to fit your style of performing. There are no rules for magic—except to make it entertaining.

CONTENTS

MAGIC ACROSS THE TABLE

1

WITH PAD AND PENCIL

LOCKED OUT

How it looks:

I'm no artist when it comes to drawing pictures," you say, "but I think that after you see this one you'll admit I do have a magic touch." You take a pad of paper from your pocket, show a pencil sketch you have made on it, and explain, "It's a picture of a door and the door is locked because the Invisible Man forgot his key and locked himself out."

You then fold the paper, tear it from the pad, put it on the table, and give your friend a metal key that you take from your pocket. He turns the key against the paper as if unlocking a door. When he opens the folded paper he finds that the door pictured on it, instead of being locked, is now wide open. "The Invisible Man thanks you," you say, "for letting him in."

The secret:

The sketch of the locked door that you first show is switched for another, which was drawn ahead of time, showing the door unlocked. One piece of paper is exchanged for the other in a simple way that makes it unnecessary to conceal anything in your hands.

Instead of the locked door, you can show a sketch of an empty flower pot and change it to one in which flowers are growing, show a sketch of an empty top hat and then show a rabbit in the hat, or show a picture of a sad face and change it to a smiling face.

What you need:

A small pad of colored paper, about 3″ × 5″, with all the sheets the same color.

A pencil to make the sketches.

A key of any kind.

How you fix it:

Turn back the top sheet of paper without tearing it from the pad. On the sheet right under it—the *second* sheet of the pad—make a simple sketch of an open door. Without tearing that sheet from the pad, fold it in half from bottom to top, crease the centerfold with your thumbnail, and then bring the top sheet of the pad down over it again. You now have what looks like an ordinary pad, because the folded second sheet is hidden under the top sheet. Both are still attached to the pad.

Now, on the top sheet, make a second sketch of the same door, but in a closed position. Put the pad into the inside breast pocket of your jacket and have the key in another pocket.

What you do:

With your left hand, take the pad from your pocket. Hold it so it rests vertically across the upturned palm of your left hand, thumb on the face of the pad and fingers

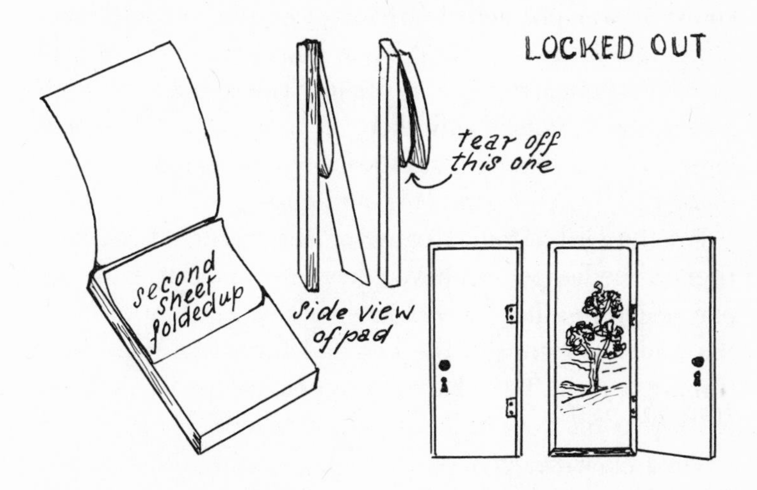

underneath. The tips of your fingers lightly hold the right edge of the pad. Turn that hand to show the face of the pad to your friend and explain that the sketch represents a locked door.

Now turn the pad so it faces you. With your right hand, fold the top sheet in half from bottom to top and crease the center fold. The folded top sheet should now be exactly over the folded second sheet beneath it.

Hold the pad upright in your left hand. Bring your

right hand to it, palm upwards. Slide your first finger under the center fold of the top sheet, and at the same time slide your second finger under the center fold of the second sheet. Grip the fold of the second sheet between your first and second fingers and tear that *second sheet* from the pad by pulling it to the right. This leaves the top sheet as it was, still attached to the pad. Hold up the folded second sheet with your right hand to display it. As you do that, turn your left hand towards your body and bring that hand up inside your jacket to drop the pad back into your inner breast pocket. The two papers have now been switched and there is nothing left for your hands to hide. The original sheet of paper is still attached to the pad, which is safely in your pocket.

Put the visible folded paper on the table and ask your friend if he happens to have a key in his pocket. If he has one, use it; but if not, give him your key. Ask him to touch the folded paper with the key and turn it as if he were turning a lock. Then have him open the paper and discover that the door in the sketch, instead of being locked, now stands wide open.

SURE WINNER

How it looks:

"Would you like to be a judge?" you ask a friend. "I want you to judge a race. It could be a boat race, a bike race, or any kind of a race. What I want you to imagine is that the race is so close the judges have to declare a winner. Let's say one of the racers is named Smith and the other named Jones. Now don't tell me yet—but in your own mind, I want you to decide who the winner is—Smith or Jones?"

You take out a pencil and pad of paper and say, "I'm going to try to predict the winner." You write a name on the paper without letting your friend see what you've written. Tear the paper from the pad, fold it, and hold the slip in your fingers. "All right," you say. "As the judge, it's time for you to declare the winner. Who won the race—Smith or Jones?" The instant he announces the name you open the slip wide and show what you have written—and your prediction is correct. The name on the paper is the name he chose. "I'll let you in on the secret," you say. "All I did was read your mind."

The secret:

One of the names has been written in advance on the back of the top sheet of the pad. When you later write your prediction, you openly write the other name on the face of the pad. The paper is folded and held in such a way that you can instantly show the correct name. It appears to be the only name on the paper.

After the trick, switch the original slip for one that bears *only* the correct name. Leave that paper on the table to satisfy your friend's curiosity in case he decides later to take a more careful look. The chances are good that he will!

What you need:

A small pad of paper and a pencil. Colored paper is best, so the writing won't show through.

How you fix it:

With the pencil, print the name "Smith" in the center of the first sheet and tear that sheet from the pad. Fold the bottom third of it up to cover the writing and crease the fold. Then fold the top third of the sheet away from you, forward and down, until what was the top edge comes to the center at the front. Crumple the paper into a loose

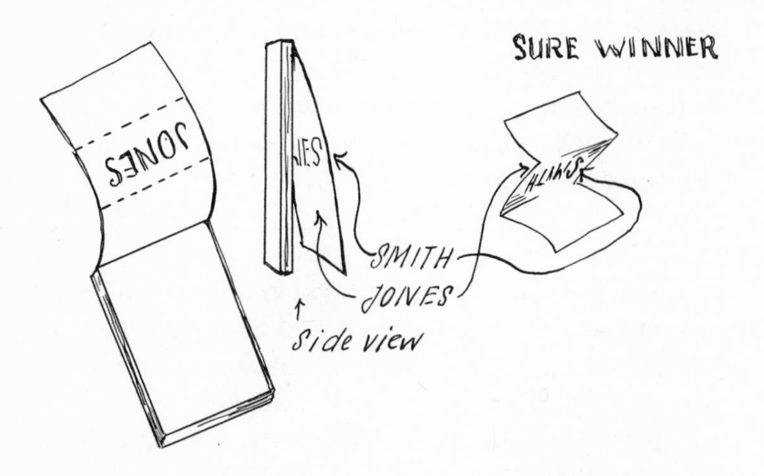

ball and put it into the right pocket of your jacket. On the second sheet, print the name "Jones," fold that as you did the first sheet, crumple it, and put it into the left pocket of your jacket.

Turn back what is now the top sheet, without removing it from the pad or turning the pad itself. At the center of the *back* of that sheet, print the name "Jones." Bring that sheet into place again at the face of the pad. You have what appears to be an ordinary pad of paper, but with the name "Jones" secretly printed on the back of the attached top sheet. If you could look through that sheet you would see that the printing is upside down. Put the pad and pencil into the right pocket of your jacket.

What you do:

When you have explained about the race and are ready to write your prediction, take the pad and pencil from your pocket. Casually show the pad and then hold it in your left hand. Bring the pad upright so your friend can't see what you are writing and print the name "Smith" at the center of the paper. Fold the bottom third of the sheet up to cover what you have written and crease the fold.

Grasp the center of the fold you have just creased between your right first finger and thumb, finger on top and thumb underneath. Tear the sheet from the upright pad. Tear from left to right and as you do, turn your right hand so the back of it is toward your friend and the thumb of that hand is toward yourself. This is the natural way you would tear the paper from the pad—but it also reverses the sheet as you remove it. Drop the pad onto the table with your left hand.

You are now holding the partly folded paper upright between your right finger and thumb, with the folded part at the front and bottom of the paper. On the side towards you, the name "Jones" shows upside down, but it can't be seen from the front. Now, with your left hand, fold the top third of the paper *down towards yourself* so that part covers the "Jones" and crease the fold.

With your left hand, take the folded slip without turning it and hold the left side of it between your thumb and first two fingers, thumb at the rear. Grasp the bottom edge of the paper, the part nearest to you, between your right first finger and thumb. You are now set to open the paper to show either the name "Smith" or the name "Jones," depending on which name your friend calls as the winner of the imaginary race.

If he calls "Jones," pull the bottom edge straight *down*, so the sheet opens out fully to reveal only that name. But if he calls "Smith," pull that bottom edge straight *up* to the top, so the paper opens out to reveal only "Smith."

Hold the paper that way a moment, then crumple it into a ball as if the trick were finished. If he has called "Jones," take the crumpled paper in your left hand, pick up the pad with the same hand, and put them both into your left pocket. Inside your pocket, switch the ball of paper in your hand for the one that has been in your pocket all along, and immediately bring your hand out. Casually drop the paper onto the table as you reach to put the pencil away. If he has called "Smith," take the pad with your right hand and switch papers in your right pocket. In either case, don't say anything about the crumpled paper you leave on the table. Let him pick it up and look it over for himself as you go on to something else.

MAP-A-MAGIC

How it looks:

"Have you seen these new tourist pencils?" you ask, as you show a pencil that you take from your pocket with a pad of paper. "With one of these you can never get lost when you're on a trip. Suppose you want to go to . . . well, let's say—Philadelphia. All you have to do is write down the name of the place."

You write the name "Philadelphia" on the pad, tear off the sheet of paper, show both sides, and fold it in half. Then you push the point of the pencil through so that the paper is impaled on the center of the pencil. "Just give the pencil a moment to work," you say, "and right away you've got a map that shows exactly which road to take." As you speak, tear the paper away and a little road map suddenly appears, hanging on the pencil. "There you are." You point to the place on the map. "The highway right into Philadelphia."

The secret:

The little map, cut from a highway travel map, is hidden in a secret pocket, formed by cementing the first two pages of the pad together so they look like one sheet of paper. When you push the pencil through the paper it also goes through the hidden map. Then, when you tear the paper away, the map is left hanging on the pencil.

What you need:

A 3″ × 5″ pad of colored paper, with pages all the same color.

A full-length, sharply-pointed pencil.

An office file card, scissors, rubber cement, a ruler, and a sheet of writing paper larger than the size of the pad.

A highway travel map, the kind given away free by gasoline service stations. One large map will serve to make many small maps for repeated showings of the trick.

How you fix it:

Cut a piece 2″ × 2″ square from the office file card and in the center of it cut a hole about ½″ in diameter. Find a part of the highway map that is printed on both sides and a section that shows roads leading to some prominent place. Make a mental note of the name of the place. You will use this name instead of "Philadelphia" when you tell the story. Cut out that part of the map so you have a piece that is slightly larger than 2″ high and 4″ wide.

Fold the piece of map in half, crease the fold, and open it out again. Coat the entire inner surface and both sides of the cardboard with rubber cement. Then put the left edge of the cardboard at the center crease of the map, and cement the map to the cardboard. When it is dry, trim the edges evenly and you will have a 2″ × 2″ piece of map, printed on both sides, with the cardboard between them for stiffening.

Take the pad and turn back the two top sheets without tearing them from the pad. Cover the third sheet of the pad with the large sheet of writing paper. This is used to keep the rubber cement from getting on the rest of the pad. Now, bring the second sheet of the pad down into place over the writing paper. Place the little map on the second sheet of the pad, centered between the two side edges and about ¼″ up from the bottom. Use the rubber cement to coat the entire right and left edges and top half of that second sheet of the pad, but leave the bottom edge uncoated. Be careful not to get any cement in the area where the map is.

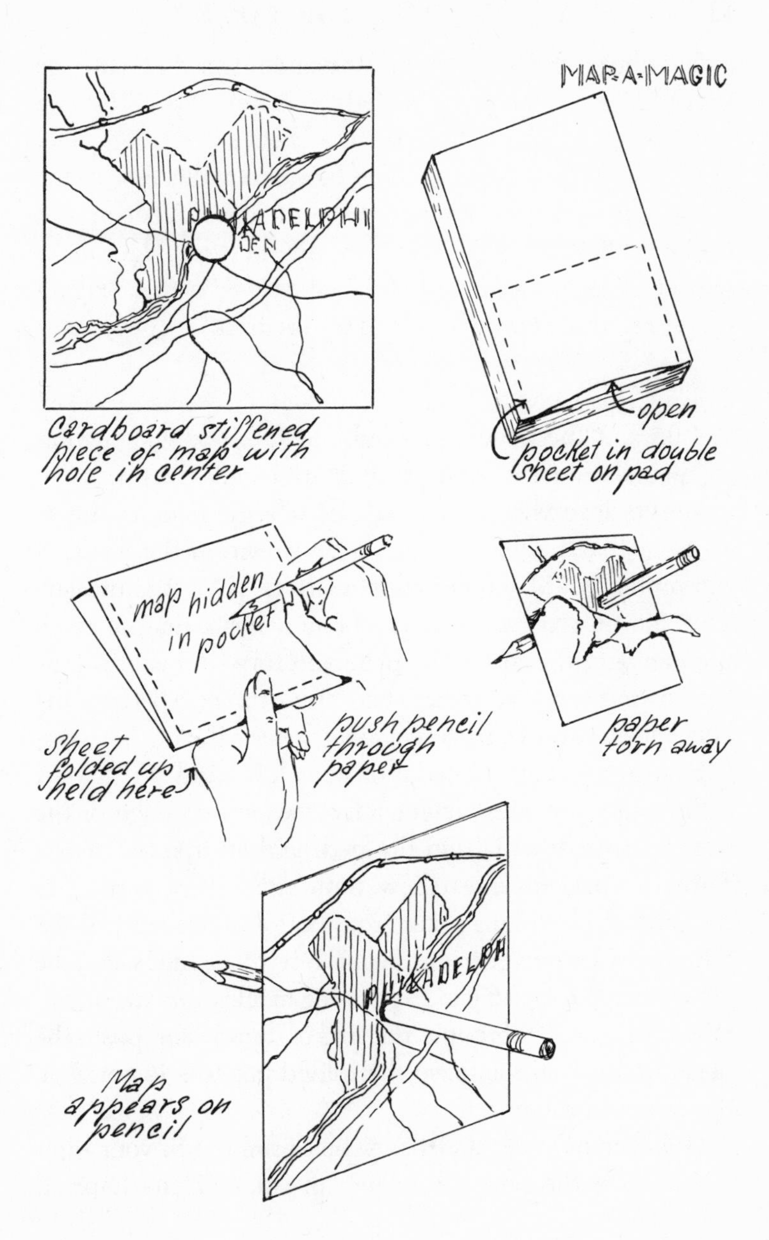
MAP-A-MAGIC
PHILADELPHI
DEN
Cardboard stiffened piece of map with hole in center
open
pocket in double sheet on pad
map hidden in pocket
push pencil through paper
Sheet folded up held here
paper torn away
PHILADELPH
Map appears on pencil

Now bring the first sheet of the pad down on top of the second sheet so that all the edges match. Press the two firmly together. Then remove the sheet of writing paper and discard it. The result should be a pad with a double top sheet that *looks* like a single piece of paper. Your map is pocketed between the sheets and the bottom edge of the pocket is open. With the pad and pencil in one of your jacket pockets, you are ready to try the trick.

What you do:

Take out the pencil and pad and talk about the "tourist" pencil. Show it as you say, "With one of these you can never get lost when you're on a trip. Suppose you want to go to . . . well, let's say. . . ." Then mention the name of the prominent place that happens to be part of your map, as if you picked the name at random. Write that name on the pad near the top of the page and turn the pad to show the writing to your friend. Then bring the pad back so the bottom edge is toward you again.

Rest the pad on the palm of your left hand. With your right thumb and first finger, take the bottom edge of the double page, tear it from the pad, and lay the pad aside. Turn the page over to show both sides, then rest it on the table and fold it in half from bottom to top. Hold the folded paper upright with your left hand and take the pencil in your right hand, gripping it close to the point. Work the point through the paper and then push the pencil halfway through, so the folded paper is impaled on the center of the pencil.

Hold the eraser end of the pencil firmly with your right hand. Turn the pencil to show all sides of the impaled paper, and finally bring it into a position so that the open ends of the paper are at the top and the center fold is at the bottom. Grip the *very edge* of the bottom fold tightly between your left first finger and thumb. With your right hand, lift the pencil straight up, ripping it through the paper. Your hidden map will suddenly appear—still impaled on the pencil.

Put the pencil, with the map on it, in front of your friend. Crumple the torn paper in your left hand and drop the pieces into your pocket as if to get rid of the scraps. Then point to the place on the map and say, "There you are—the main highway into (whatever town you named before.)"

TRACER

How it looks:

You borrow a quarter from your friend and put it on the table with a pad and pencil that you take from your pocket. "Sometimes things vanish without a trace," you say. "I wouldn't want that to happen to your quarter, so I'll make a tracing of it." You put the quarter under the top sheet of the pad and rub the pencil over it to make a clear tracing of the coin. Then you drop the coin from the pad to the table and cover the coin with the pad.

"There's the picture of your quarter," you say, as you point to the tracing. "But where's the quarter?" When he tells you it is under the pad on the table, you ask, "Are you sure?" He looks for himself but he discovers that under the pad, instead of his quarter, there is a five-cent piece.

"At least it didn't disappear without a trace," you say. "It just shrank a little. . . . But don't worry. I'll give you one of mine." You reach into your pocket, take out a quarter and hand it to him, as you assure him: "This one won't vanish. It's pre-shrunk."

The secret:

The bottom page of the pad is cemented to the cardboard backing to form a pocket where the nickel is hidden at the start. As you trace the quarter, you let it slide sidewise into your hand, and it is the hidden nickel that you drop onto the table and quickly cover with the pad. It is his own quarter, which has been concealed in your hand, that you pretend to take from your pocket when you give him "another quarter" to replace the money you borrowed.

What you need:

A pad of colored paper about 3″ × 5″ in size, which has the usual cardboard backing, and a soft lead pencil.

A nickel.

Rubber cement.

How to fix it:

Open the pad to the last sheet of paper. Lift that and, with the rubber cement, coat a horizontal strip across the cardboard backing about 1½″ up from its bottom edge and then coat a vertical strip at each side. Smooth the sheet of paper down so it sticks to the cardboard and forms a little pocket in which you can hide the nickel. The pocket is open at the bottom. If you tilt the pad upright the nickel will drop out.

Slide the nickel into its hiding place, close the rest of the pad, and put the pad *with its bottom end up* into the breast pocket of your jacket. Have the pencil in the same pocket.

What you do:

Ask your friend if he has a quarter you can borrow and have him put it on the table. Take the pad and pencil from your pocket and rest them on the table a moment as you let it be seen, without saying so, that your hands are empty.

Hold your left hand palm upwards in front of you, fingertips toward the right. Put the pad on that hand so it lies vertically on your fingers, with the left edge of it toward your palm, and rest the back of that hand on the table.

With your right hand, turn back the top sheet of the pad. Pick up the quarter, place it on the center of the pad, and pause long enough so that the coin may be clearly seen there. Drop the top sheet back over it and press your left thumb lightly to the edge of the coin through the paper to keep it in position.

Take the pencil with your right hand and gently rub the point back and forth over the coin to trace it through the paper. As you trace, raise your left fingers slightly and tilt the pad to the side. This will allow the quarter to slide to the left edge of the pad, with the paper still covering it. The quarter, under the covering paper, should slide against the base of your left thumb. But continue to work the pencil with your right hand as if still tracing the outline of the coin.

Put the pencil down. Bring your right first finger and

thumb to the top right corner of the pad. Slide the pad away to the right to draw it out of your left hand. That leaves the quarter in your left hand. Your fingers loosely close around it as you immediately turn that hand over and rest it on the table. Focus attention on the pad by holding it up in your right hand. Give it a little shake so the nickel falls out to the table. Without pausing drop the pad on top of the nickel to cover it.

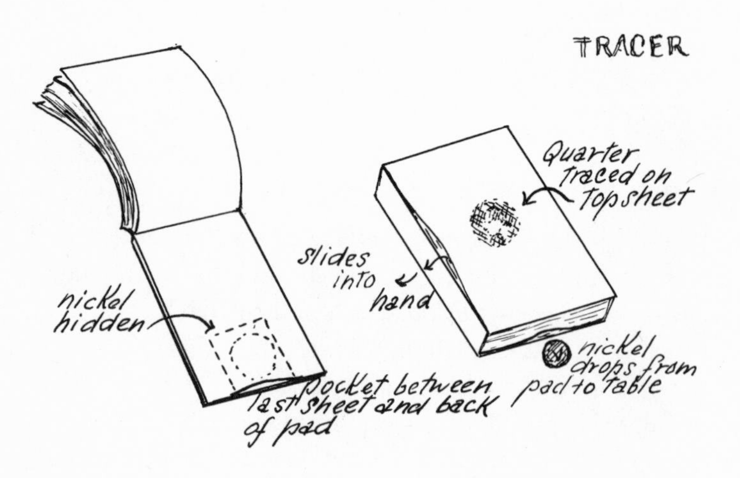

This gives your friend only a momentary glimpse of a shiny coin falling to the table before the pad covers it. You want him to think is that you merely tipped the pad to slide out the quarter you were tracing. As far as he knows, this is the only coin in use.

Ask him where the quarter is. Have him lift the pad and discover the nickel instead of the quarter. "At least it didn't disappear without a trace. It just shrank a little," you tell him. "But don't worry. I'll give you one of mine." With your left hand still concealing the quarter, reach into your pocket. Pretend to search a little and then bring the same quarter out again and give it back to him as you say, "This one won't vanish. It's pre-shrunk."

2

WITH BOTTLE CAPS

POP GOES THE BOTTLE

How it looks:

"Do you happen to have a bottle opener in your pocket?" you ask a friend while you search your own pockets as if looking for one. "Never mind," you say, "because I haven't got a bottle to open." You hold your empty hands in front of you, stare down at them and shake your head, then drop your hands to your sides. "But if I did have a bottle—then I would need a bottle opener—"

You raise your left hand as if holding a bottle and bring your right hand over as if using a bottle opener. "If I did have a bottle, then I would need an opener—because how else would I get off the cap?" As you pretend to open the imaginary bottle, a real bottle cap pops from your hand high into the air.

The secret:

Meant to amuse more than to amaze, this simple little magical surprise depends on getting a bottle cap into your sleeve so it will slide into your hand at the right moment.

What you need and how you fix it:

All you need is the bottle cap, which you carry in the right pocket of your jacket.

What you do:

Ask your friend if he happens to have a bottle opener and begin to search your own pockets. Put your right hand into your jacket pocket, conceal the bottle cap in your fingers, bring the hand out, and reach up under the left side of your jacket to pat the pocket of your shirt. As you do that, your left hand grips the left lapel of your jacket to pull it out a little, which provides a logical excuse for keeping your left arm bent upwards from the elbow. With your right hand under your jacket, drop the bottle cap into the top of your left sleeve. Because your left arm is bent, the cap falls down that sleeve only as far as the elbow.

Keeping your left elbow bent, immediately pat under the right side of your jacket with your left hand, and then bring both hands out in front of you. Hold them palms upward, fingers apart, stare down at your hands, and shake your head. Then drop both hands to your sides as you say, "But if I did have a bottle—then I would need a bottle opener—"

The fingers of your left hand fall into a natural cuplike position at your side as the bottle cap drops down out of the sleeve into that hand. Now turn a little to the right and bring your left hand up in front of you, loosely formed into a half-open fist as if it were holding the neck of an imaginary bottle. The back of your hand is toward those watching.

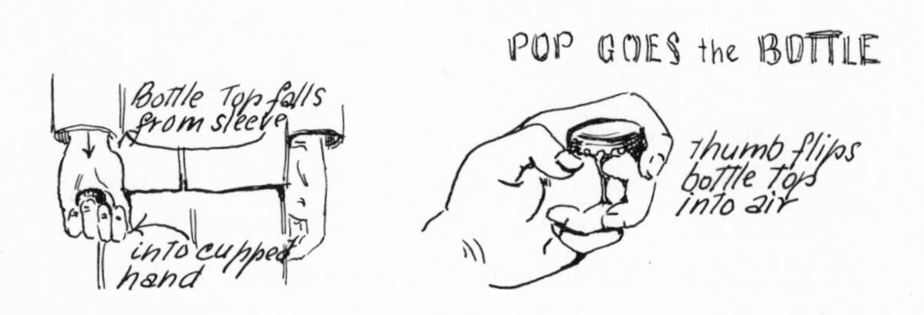

As you repeat the words, "If I did have a bottle, then I would need an opener," bring your left thumb down inside your hand under the edge of the bottle cap, and bring your right hand over as if it held an opener. Go through the final motion of opening the imaginary bottle and ask, "Because how else would I get off the cap?"

Snap your left thumb straight up and flip the cap high into the air, exactly as you would flip a coin. Make a popping sound with your mouth and pretend to look as surprised as your friend should be as your eyes follow the cap when it flies up and then falls to the floor.

NO DEPOSIT—NO RETURN

How it looks:

"Most of the bottles of soda you buy these days are marked 'No deposit—no return,'" you say, "but I've discovered that isn't true of the caps from those bottles." Give a friend a marking pen and ask him to mark his initials inside a bottle cap. From your pocket, you take an empty paper matchbox, open it, and put the bottle cap into it. Close the box and put it to one side of the table. Then you take another matchbox from your pocket and put that at the other side of the table.

You pick up the box containing his marked bottle cap. "No deposit," you say. You crush the box flat and tear it into small pieces, which you drop to the table. The bottle cap has vanished. "But they do return," you say, and point to the other matchbox. Invite him to open it. Inside he finds the missing bottle cap with his initials on it.

The secret:

The first paper matchbox has no bottom in it. When you put the bottle cap into the box it goes right through into your hand. In your pocket, the second matchbox has its drawer open. When you reach into your pocket to remove it, you just put the hidden bottle cap into it and close it before bringing it out. The simple trickery is all over before the trick seems to begin, and the rest is merely a matter of acting it out.

What you need:

Two empty pocket-sized paper matchboxes, not *folders* of matches but *boxes* of the kind that once were made of wood but now generally thin cardboard.

A bottle cap, a felt-tip marking pen, and a pair of scissors.

How to fix it:

Use the scissors to cut away about five-sixths of the bottom from the sliding drawer of one of the paper matchboxes. Trim the edges cleanly so you can gently slide the drawer in and out without difficulty. Slide the drawer inside the cover. With the pen, put a tiny mark on the cover at the end where the drawer is bottomless so you can tell that end at a glance.

Slide the drawer of the second matchbox open almost all the way and put that box on its side in the left pocket of your jacket, with the open drawer facing away from your body. Put the closed bottomless matchbox into the same pocket and have the bottle cap and marking pen handy in other pockets.

What you do:

Take out the bottle cap, show it, and give it to your friend. Hand him the marking pen and ask him to print his initials, as large as possible, inside the cap. Put the pen away and say, "I have a matchbox in my pocket." Remove the bottomless box from your left pocket, turn it over casually to show both sides, and then rest the box crosswise on the upturned fingers of your left hand.

Tilt your left hand upwards slightly and with your right hand slide back the cover and open the box. Pick up the bottle cap with your right hand, show it, and slowly and openly put it into the box, so it goes right through the bottom and is gripped by your cupped left fingers. Put your right thumb at the bottom end of the box, your right fingers at the top, and gently slide the box shut. Keep the box gripped between your right thumb and fingers, lift it

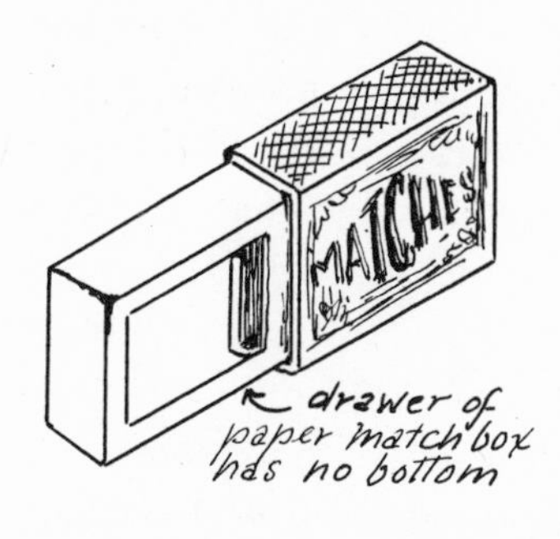

NO DEPOSIT-NO RETURN

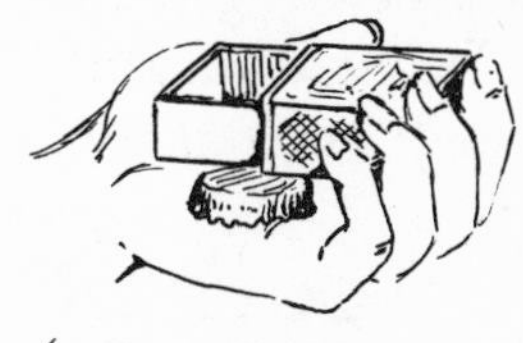

bottle cap goes right through open bottom into palm of hand

away from your left hand, and look toward the box as you place it on the table to the right. Let your left hand, with the bottle cap concealed in your fingers, fall to your side for a moment.

Say, "I have another matchbox in my pocket." Reach into your left pocket with your left hand. With your hand inside your pocket, without any hurried movement, bring the bottle cap against the open drawer so the cap goes into the box. Slide the box shut. Without rattling it, bring the box out and gently place it at the left of the table.

Point to the box at your right and ask, "Do you remember the color of that bottle cap?" Take that box and hold it between both hands, thumbs at the rear, fingers at the front, and say, "No deposit." Push your thumbs up and crush the box flat, then tear it into halves. Hold one half in each hand a moment and say, "Whatever color it was, it is now invisible—the bottle cap has gone." Tear the rest of the paper box into pieces and let them flutter down to the table. Brush your hands together and say: "All gone."

Now turn your head to the left and stare down at the box at that side of the table. Look up, smile, and nod your head. "But they do return," you say. Point to the box without touching it and say, "Open it yourself. Look inside." As he takes out the bottle cap, ask: "Is that the same one? Are your initials in it?"

CHOOSER'S CHOICE

How it looks:

Take an envelope from your pocket, remove three bottle caps from it, and place them in a row on the table. One is the cap from a bottle of grape soda, the second from a bottle of cola, the third from a bottle of orange. From another pocket, take out a handful of small change. Select a quarter from among the coins and put that on the table next to the three bottle caps. You then ask your friend to take the quarter and place it on top of any one of the three bottle caps.

"Would you like to change your mind?" you ask. He may do so if he wishes. When he finally leaves the coin on top of one of the three caps, you ask, "Are you convinced you had an absolutely free choice? . . . Well, you're wrong. I made up your mind for you. I cast a magic spell so that you would choose the one I wanted you to choose." If he has chosen the cap from the bottle of orange soda, for instance, you say, "Just turn over the quarter." When he turns it over, he finds cemented to the other side of the coin a little circle of paper, on which are the words: "YOU WILL CHOOSE ORANGE."

The secret:

This is a trick you cannot do twice for the same friend or group of friends because its secret depends on the chooser not knowing in advance how it will end. You end it according to which of the three bottle caps is chosen, but with things secretly arranged so that it always seems he has chosen the one cap you wanted him to choose.

What you need:

Three soda bottle caps. Each should be clearly marked with its flavor, such as grape, cola and orange, but any three that are different may be used.

A small business envelope that is not transparent.

Two slips of paper, scissors, liquid adhesive, and a pen.

A quarter and a few nickels, dimes and pennies.

How you fix it:

On one of the paper slips print: YOU WILL CHOOSE GRAPE. Put it into the envelope.

From the other slip of paper cut two small circular pieces, one slightly smaller than the size of the quarter, the other just large enough to fit inside a bottle cap so that when it is pressed into place it will stay there.

On the coin-sized paper circle write, one word to a line: YOU WILL CHOOSE ORANGE. Cement that circle firmly to one side of the quarter and trim the edges so none of the paper shows when the quarter is turned over. On the other circle, one word to a line, write: YOU WILL CHOOSE COLA. Press it firmly into place inside the cola bottle cap.

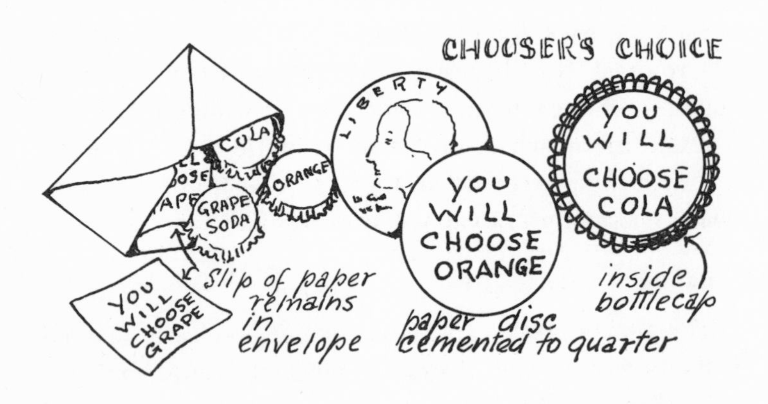

Put the three caps into the envelope which contains the slip of paper, and have it in a jacket pocket. Carry the quarter and the rest of the small change in another pocket.

What you do:

Take the envelope from your pocket and remove the three bottle caps one at a time, making sure that the printed crown is facing up before you take it from the envelope. Put them in a row on the table and drop the envelope to one side of the table.

Reach into the pocket where you have the loose

empty space." You reach into another pocket and say, "Oh, here they are," as you remove two bottle caps, one red and the other blue, and toss them onto the table. "They may look like bottle caps to you," you say, "but they're really flying saucers—for invisible little men."

Pick up the blue one, show it, and slowly put it into your right jacket pocket. "I'll put the blue one in this space pocket." Then you pick up the red one and put it into the left pocket of your jacket. "And I'll put the red one in *this* space pocket."

Now you ask your watching friend, "Do you remember which space pocket the blue one was in? Will you please reach into my pocket and take it out?" He reaches into your right pocket but finds the red one there instead of the blue. You invite him to reach into your left pocket and he discovers the blue one instead of the red. "You see, they *are* space ships," you say, "and they travel so fast you can't see them whizz across—faster than the speed of light."

You then have him put them on the table and say, "We'll try another flight." You pick up the blue one and put it into your right pocket. "Remember the blue one is in this space pocket." Then you take the red one and put it into your left pocket. "Remember the red one is in this space pocket." Now you invite him to reach into your pocket and remove the red one. When he searches your left pocket this time he discovers nothing at all. The pocket is empty. "This time it was a duo-flight," you say. "They both flew over here. Look for yourself." He puts his hand into your right pocket and finds both the red and the blue are there together.

Have him put both caps on the table again. "Let's try a long-distance flight," you say. "Will you please empty the things out of your pocket?" He empties one of his jacket pockets. You pick up the blue cap and put it into his pocket. Then you drop the red one into your pocket. "Now which space saucer is in my pocket?" you ask.

When he says the red one is, you say, "No—they've flown across again. I have the blue one." You take it from your pocket and toss it onto the table. "Which means, of course, that you must have the red." He looks in his pocket and finds the red one there instead of the blue. "They're pretty clever astronauts," you say. "Those invisible little men."

The secret:

There are really three bottle caps, not two, but you handle them in such a way that nobody guesses you have a duplicate red. The extra red cap is hidden in your hand and switched for one or the other inside the pockets, which conceal the change. Since your friend searches both your pockets and his and handles the two caps himself he has no reason to suspect the use of a third one.

What you need:

Three bottle caps, two red ones which look alike and one blue, or caps of any other contrasting colors.

How you fix it:

Empty both pockets of your jacket. Put one red bottle cap in the right pocket. Have the other two, one red and one blue, in the right pocket of your trousers.

What you do:

Put your right hand into the jacket pocket on that side and your left hand into the other pocket. Close your right fingers loosely around the bottle cap to conceal it. Grip the bottom lining of the pocket and pull it straight up and out, turning it inside out. Hold it that way a moment before pushing the lining back in again. Leave the bottle cap in the pocket as you remove your hand. Meanwhile your left hand pulls its pocket inside out and pushes it back in the same way at the same time.

Pat your trousers pockets with both hands as if searching for the "space saucers." With your right hand, take out the other two bottle caps and put them on the table. Casually let it be seen that your hands are empty.

With your right hand, pick up the blue bottle cap and pretend to put it into the pocket of your jacket on that side, but as soon as your hand is inside the pocket just close your fingers around the cap and immediately bring your hand out again with the cap concealed in it. Now, with the same hand pick the red cap up from the table, holding it between your thumb and first finger. While your left hand holds your left-hand pocket open, bring your right hand across and put it into your left pocket. But as soon as your hand is inside the pocket, open your fingers and let the blue cap they have been hiding fall into the pocket. Then close your fingers to conceal the red cap and bring your hand out again.

Drop both hands to your sides, with one red cap still hidden in the fingers of your right hand. Ask your friend which pocket the blue one is in and when he says it is in your right pocket invite him to reach into that pocket and take it out. Instead of the blue one he expects to find, he discovers the red one that has been in that pocket from the start. Now have him reach into your other pocket and take out the blue cap instead of the red one he thought was there.

Have him put both caps on the table again. Pick up the blue cap and put it into the far front of your right pocket and then put the red one your hand has been hiding into the rear part of that pocket. Do it slowly, keeping the two caps apart so there is no sound. Bring your hand out, let it be seen that it is empty, and pick up the red cap from the table.

While your left hand holds the pocket at its side open, bring your right hand across as if to put the red cap into your left pocket. As soon as your right hand is inside that pocket, close your fingers around the red cap to hide it, and immediately bring your hand out again. You just pretend to put the cap into that pocket but you really put nothing there.

Ask your friend which pocket the red one is in. When he says it is in your left pocket, invite him to reach in and remove it. He will find the pocket empty. Then invite him to reach into your right pocket, where he finds that both caps have "flown together." Ask him to put them both on the table once more. There is still a red cap hidden in your right hand.

Have him empty his jacket pocket for the "long-distance flight." With your right hand, which has a red one hidden in it, pick up the blue one from the table and tell him you will put that one in his pocket. But when your hand is inside his pocket, drop the hidden red one instead, and bring your hand out with the blue one hidden in it. Pick up the red one from the table and drop that into your right pocket, still keeping the blue one hidden in your hand.

Ask him which one is in your pocket. He will say red. Reach in and bring out the blue one that has been hidden in your hand and toss it on the table. When he reaches into his own pocket he finds red instead of blue. You end as you started, with two bottle caps visible, your hands empty, and the unsuspected third cap safely hidden away in your right pocket.

3

WITH CHEWING GUM

IF I HAD A SAW

How it looks:

If I had a saw in my pocket, and a woman, I'd show you how to saw a woman in two," you say. "But since I haven't a saw in my pocket, or a woman, I can give you only a rough idea of what it looks like."

You remove a stick of chewing gum from a pack, tear the stick into two pieces, hold one half in each hand, and then put the two together and show that the stick is restored again as one piece, which you unwrap to prove that it has suffered no harm.

The secret:

There is an empty wrapper, which looks like a full stick of gum, attached to the real stick. When you tear the paper wrapper in half it looks as if you had torn the gum in two.

What you need:

Two identical sticks of gum from a freshly opened pack. Stale gum cannot be used because one of the sticks must be flexible enough to be bent double without breaking it.

Rubber cement or other adhesive.

How you fix it:

Slide one foil-wrapped stick of gum from its outer paper wrapper. Remove the gum, refold the empty foil as it was when it contained the gum, and then slide the foil

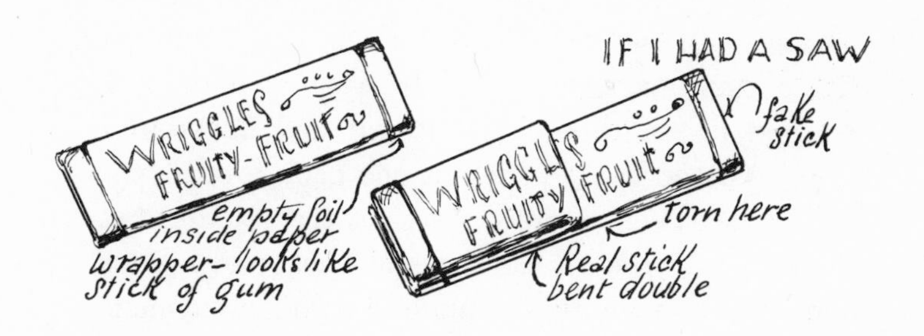

back into the outer wrapper again. You should have what outwardly looks exactly like a stick of gum but with no gum inside it.

Put the other wrapped stick of gum lengthwise on a table. Coat the right half of it from the center to the end, including the foil tip, with rubber cement, and then fasten the faked one to the face of it. The two should be firmly cemented at the right half and all edges should exactly match. Press it down to flatten it as much as you can and round the sides and edges with your thumb and fingers. Put the double stick back into the pack, so that the cemented end is toward the open end of the pack. Keep it in the right pocket of your jacket.

What you do:

Take the pack of gum from your pocket with your right hand and bring the left hand over to draw out the faked stick. Grip the end of the stick between your left first finger and thumb, with your thumb underneath. Turn the stick vertically upright, so you are holding it with finger and thumb at the bottom, finger to the front and thumb at the rear. With your right hand, drop the rest of the pack back into your pocket and leave it there.

Bring your right hand over to the top of the upright stick of gum and grip the top between your right thumb and first finger, thumb at the rear and finger in front. Now bend the double stick as one back toward yourself until it has been doubled back so the top touches the bottom. Hold the tip of the real stick under your left thumb. With your right thumb and finger, immediately bend just the front part, the empty wrapper, up straight again. The impression you want to give is that you merely bent the stick double and then straightened it out so as to make it easier to tear.

Rip the empty front wrapper in half across its center by pulling your right first finger and thumb back and toward the right. Separate your hands and hold them apart to show what appears to be half the stick of gum in each hand. Then bring the right hand over to the left and put the part that the right hand holds in front of the part in your left. Even up the sides of the two pieces and move them down inside the fingers of your left hand.

Behind the fingers of your left hand, and with the help of your left thumb, quickly straighten out the stick of gum. Lower your left hand so it is palm upwards, press your left thumb on the end nearest to you to help conceal the torn wrapper beneath it, and display the apparently restored stick of gum on the palm of your left hand.

With your right first finger and thumb, grip the end of the foil and draw the foil-wrapped stick out of the paper wrapper. Crumple the wrapper in your left hand. With both hands, open up the foil to show the unharmed inner stick of gum. Then crumple the foil into your left hand with the wrapper and drop them both into your left pocket. Hold up the unwrapped gum and say, "There she is—just as good as new," as you put it into your mouth to chew it.

GUMGO

How it looks:

This little pantomime in mystery, for which no talk is necessary, is a simple and direct vanishing of a stick of chewing gum. You show a small square of newspaper, fold it in half diagonally so it forms a triangle, and put it on the table. From a pack of gum, remove one stick which you place on the paper. You slowly wrap the gum in the paper. When you pull the paper open, the gum has disappeared, and you crumple up the paper as final proof that it really has vanished.

The secret:

What looks like a stick of gum really is only the empty wrapper, fixed to look that way. The newspaper is folded and opened so the gum seems to vanish from sight. Actually it is hidden under the paper, between it and the table top, and then crumpled up inside the paper.

What you need:

A pack of chewing gum.
A 6″ square cut from a sheet of newspaper.

How you fix it:

Take a stick of gum from the pack, remove the gum from the foil, refold the foil as it was and slide it back into the paper wrapper, so it again looks like a stick of gum but has no gum inside it. Put this faked stick into the pack.

Put the square of newspaper on a table and turn the top right corner of the square to the right side so that the square is in a diamond-shaped position—one corner pointing toward your waist, the opposite corner directly away from you. Take the corner that points toward your waist and bring it up to within about ¼″ of the corner that points away from you, and crease the paper across the center fold.

You now should have a triangle, with its base at the bottom and its apex at the top. The point of the upper fold is about ¼″ shorter than the point of the under fold. Now turn the whole paper over from right to left so that the shorter fold is underneath. That is in the position it should be in when you wrap up the stick of gum. Remember that the short fold should always be underneath.

Put the square of newspaper, folded as a triangle, into the inner breast pocket of your jacket. Have the pack of gum, with the faked stick on top of the real sticks, in the left pocket of your jacket.

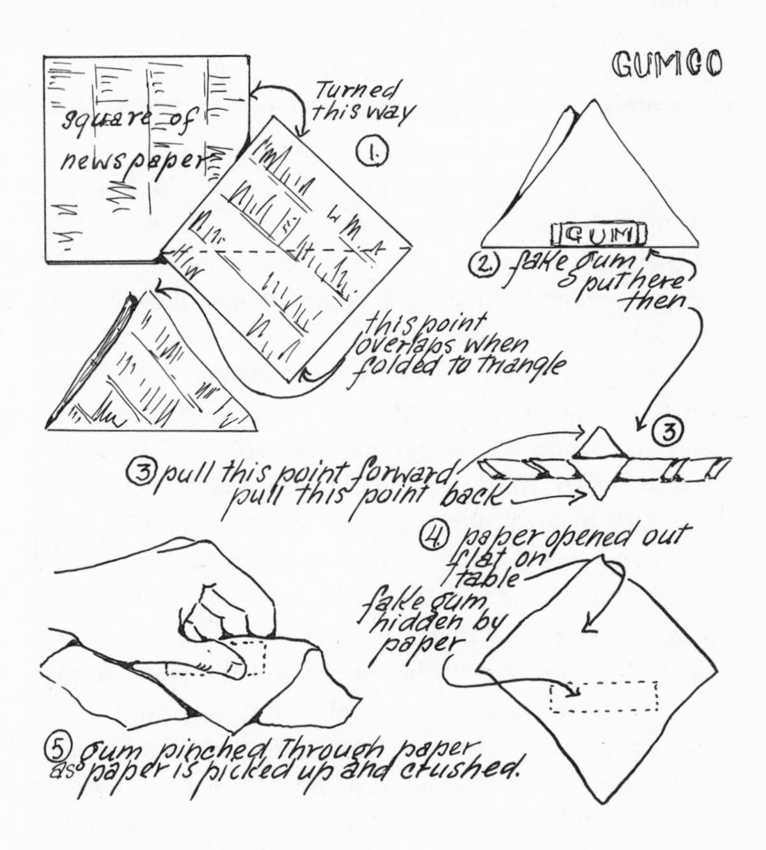

What you do:

Remove the pack of gum, draw out the faked stick, put it on the table to your right, and drop the pack back into your pocket. Take out the piece of newspaper, hold it open to show it, and refold it on its crease. Put the folded triangle of paper at the center of the table with its base toward you. Remember: the shorter fold is underneath, against the surface of the table.

Show the faked wrapper as a stick of gum. Put it on the base of the paper triangle, horizontally, so it is centered there, and lift your hands away for a moment so the gum may be clearly seen. Keep the paper on the table and fold it up around the gum, starting from the base and wrapping the paper upward, away from you. Keep folding the paper over and over, four times, and then turn it over once more so that both points of the triangle come into view.

Without lifting the paper from the surface of the table, grip the point of the triangle that is nearest to you between your left first finger and thumb. Grip the other point between your right first finger and thumb. With your right hand, pull the paper straight forward on the table to open it out fully. Press your right thumb to the far point and your left thumb to the rear point to hold the opened paper flat on the table.

The paper appears to be empty and the stick of gum seems to have vanished. Actually it is underneath the paper at the center, between the paper and the table top. Hold it that way a second and then pinch the center of the paper with your right hand, feeling through the paper to take the gum wrapper with it. Crumple the paper and hidden wrapper into your right hand. Crush it into a tight little ball. Show the paper ball on the palm of your right hand, toss it to your left hand, show it there, and drop it into your left pocket. Brush your hands together, hold them out in front of you, and then shrug your shoulders as you let your hands fall to your sides.

Crumpling up the paper with the gum wrapper hidden in it should be practiced so you can do it quickly and smoothly. For practice, you can straighten out the crumpled wrapper and re-use it, but of course you must have a fresh one when you show the trick. It should look like a real stick of gum.

WHICH CHEW FOR YOU?

How it looks:

"Would you like some chewing gum?" you ask, as you take out a yellow-wrapped pack and give a stick of it to your friend. As you remove another yellow-wrapped stick for yourself, you say, "I don't like this kind much." You pass your hand over it and the yellow changes to a green-wrapped stick. Shaking your head, you look at it and say, "I don't like that kind, either." You pass your hand over it once more and the stick that was yellow and then green changes to white. "There," you say. "That's the kind I like best."

The secret:

The stick of gum has a faked wrapper, all white on one side and with a flap on the other side that shows first yellow and then green.

What you need:

Three packs of chewing gum, all with sticks the same size, and each with a paper wrapper of a different color, such as Juicy Fruit, Doublemint and Spearmint.

Rubber cement or other adhesive, and a pair of scissors.

How you fix it:

Remove one stick from the yellow-wrapped pack. Slide the foil-wrapped gum from its wrapper and cut the paper wrapper apart along each of its horizontal sides. Take one of the pieces you have cut and put it lengthwise on a table with the printing right side up. Fold it exactly in half from right to left, so the two short edges meet at the left end, and crease it across the center with your thumbnail. Now bend the folded part far enough back to the right so that it stands straight up from the center.

Leave that for a moment and do the same thing with a green paper wrapper. You now should have two L-shaped half-wrappers, one yellow and the other green. With rubber cement, coat the upright *unprinted* white parts of each of them. Bring those two upright parts together, back to back, and press them firmly so they are cemented to each other.

Take a stick of gum from the white-wrapped pack and coat the face of that stick with rubber cement along its whole lengthwise surface. Stick the base of the yellow-green wrapper directly over the white one so both ends match. When the cement is dry, trim all the edges with the scissors.

When you have finished fixing it, the stick should have a double yellow-green flap on its face and an all-white label at the back. If you fold the flap all the way in one direction it looks like a yellow-wrapped stick; if you fold it the other way it looks green-wrapped; if you turn the stick over it appears to be white-wrapped. Turn the flap to its yellow face and put it back into the yellow-wrapped pack, with the open end of the flap toward the open end of the pack. Put a plain stick of yellow-wrapped gum into the pack on top of the trick one and have the pack in the left pocket of your jacket.

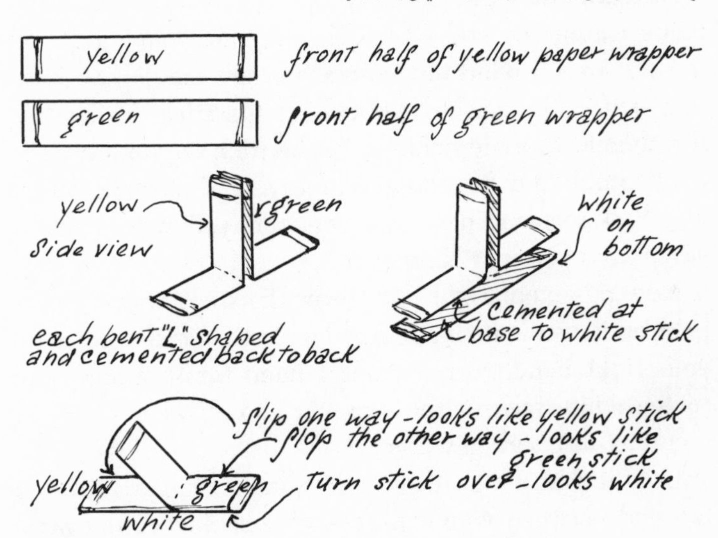

What you do:

Take the pack from your pocket with your left hand. With your right hand, remove the ordinary stick of gum and give that to your friend. Grip the faked end of the next stick between your right thumb and first two fingers, thumb on top to hold down the flap, and draw it out of the pack. Drop the rest of the pack back into your pocket with your left hand.

Hold the stick about at waist level in front of you, gripped as it was between your right thumb and fingers. Show your left hand empty and bring it palm downwards until it is about an inch above the stick of gum, covering it from view from the top.

Draw your right thumb back slightly to release the end of the flap. It will spring up a little to touch your left palm. Catch the end of the flap against your palm and move your left hand to the left to swing the flap over. As your left hand reaches the end of the stick, bring your left thumb up underneath, grip the stick of gum between your thumb and fingers, and take your right hand away. The stick seems to have changed from yellow to green as you passed your left hand over it.

Now pass your right hand over the stick, which is still held as it was with your left hand. Under the cover of your right hand, turn your left hand forward and over so the white face of the wrapper shows. The stick now seems to have turned white.

Hold it that way with your left hand. Grip the silvered foil end between your right thumb and fingers and draw the stick of gum out of its wrapper. With your left hand put the wrapper into your pocket, then peel the foil from the gum and put that into the same pocket. Put the gum into your mouth to chew it as you say to your friend, with a smile, "If you want to change yours into Spearmint, go ahead—I don't mind."

THROUGH AND THROUGH

How it looks:

Show a stick of chewing gum, a quarter, and a flat cardboard tube that is open at both ends. When you drop the quarter into the top of the tube, it slides through and falls out the bottom. But there is a crosswise slot at the center of the tube and when you insert the gum in that it blocks the tube so the quarter can't slide through.

"This chewing gum has a lot of imagination," you say. "It imagines itself being chewed, so that it pulls apart and sticks itself back together again—so fast you can't see it happen." You drop the quarter back into the top of the tube and it seems to pass right through the stick of gum so that it falls out the bottom.

"That's a pretty clever stick of gum," you say, as you do it once more. Again the quarter seems to pass right through the flat stick of gum that blocks the center of the tube. "It has every reason to be proud of itself." Hand your friend the tube, the quarter, and the chewing gum. "But you can see for yourself that it isn't a bit stuck up."

The secret:

Your friend thinks only one quarter is used, but there is a duplicate quarter which is hidden at the start of the trick in a secret compartment of the tube. When you drop the visible quarter into the top, that one stays there, and it is the hidden second quarter that falls out at the bottom. Since both coins look alike it seems as if the same quarter slid through the tube and the stick of gum that blocks the center. Your audience sees only one coin at a time and has no reason to guess that the tube hides a second quarter. By reversing the tube, you repeat the trick.

What you need:

A wrapped stick of chewing gum.
Two quarters that look alike.
A 3″ × 5″ office file card.
Scissors and rubber cement or other adhesive.

How you fix it:

With the file card lengthwise on a table, fold the left edge to the center, crease the fold, and then fold it to the right again and to the right once more, creasing each of those folds. That gives you a card with four sections divided by three vertical creases.

Open out the card. In the third section, immediately to the right of the center, rest one of the quarters about ¼″ down from the top of the card. Just below the bottom edge of the coin, coat a horizontal stripe of rubber cement. Remove the quarter, coat the entire fourth section of the card with rubber cement, and then fold the card from left to right on its creases, pressing firmly as you fold so that you have a flat cardboard tube.

When the rubber cement is dry, make a horizontal slot right through the tube across the center, long enough and wide enough so that you can slide the flat stick of gum into the slot.

Squeeze the sides of the tube to open it up a little. If

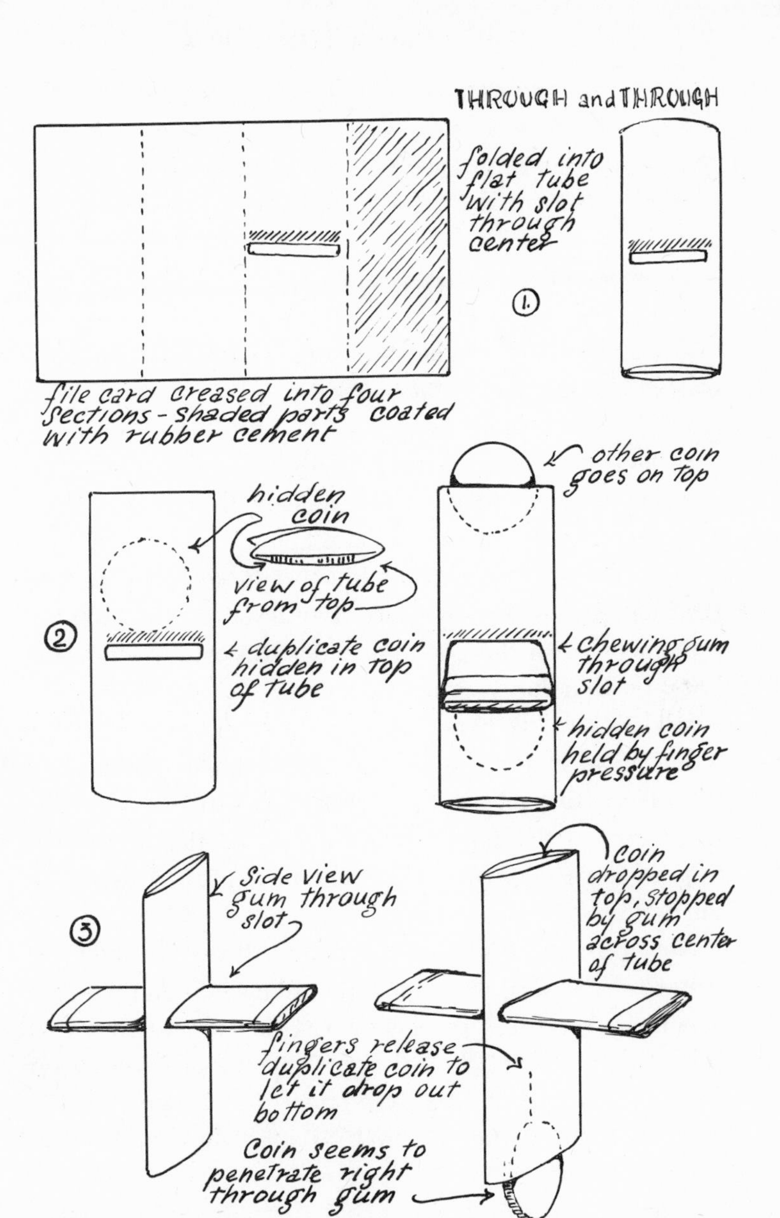
THROUGH and THROUGH
folded into flat tube with slot through center
1.
file card creased into four sections - shaded parts coated with rubber cement
2
hidden coin
view of tube from top
duplicate coin hidden in top of tube
other coin goes on top
chewing gum through slot
hidden coin held by finger pressure
3
side view gum through slot
coin dropped in top, stopped by gum across center of tube
fingers release duplicate coin to let it drop out bottom
Coin seems to penetrate right through gum

you examine the top you will see there is a fold of cardboard between the side and center. A quarter hidden there will not drop on through the tube because that section is cemented at the bottom just above the center slot.

Hide one of the quarters in that part of the tube, keep the tube upright, and put it into the outer breast pocket of your jacket. Have the duplicate quarter and the stick of gum in one of your other pockets.

What you do:

Take the stick of gum and quarter from your pocket and put them on the table. Then take the cardboard tube from your breast pocket, holding it in such a way that the hidden coin stays in place. Lay it flat on the table for a moment, with the end that hides the coin toward you. Let it be seen that your hands are empty.

With your left hand, pick up the tube again so the hidden coin is at the top. Squeeze the sides to open up the tube a little. With your right hand, take the visible quarter from the table and drop it into the top of the tube so it goes down through the center and falls out at the bottom.

Now push the flat stick of gum halfway through the crosswise slot. Grip the top of the tube so the hidden coin is held by the pressure of your left fingers and turn that end of the tube to the bottom. Drop the visible quarter into what is now the top and show that it does not fall through because the flat stick of gum through the slot blocks the way.

Still gripping the hidden coin through the cardboard at the bottom, tilt the tube to drop the visible quarter back into your right hand. Hold the tube upright once more. Drop the visible quarter into the top again, release the pressure of your fingers at the bottom, and let the hidden coin fall out. It looks as though the quarter passed through the stick of gum.

With your right thumb and first finger, grip the top end of the tube, pressing to hold the other quarter, which is now hidden there. Reverse the tube to bring that end to the bottom. With your left hand, pick up the quarter from the table. Drop it into the top of the tube, at the same time easing the grip of your finger and thumb at the bottom. The other coin will fall out to the table, and it seems that for a second time a quarter has passed through the gum.

You still have a coin hidden in the top of the tube. Hold the tube at the bottom with your left hand. Bring your right hand to the top so all four fingers are in front and your thumb is at the rear and transfer the tube to that hand. Turn the tube over so your right palm is cupped beneath it and let the hidden coin fall into that hand, concealed from the front by your fingers. With your left hand, pull the stick of gum from the slot and drop it onto the table.

Holding the tube again with your left hand, let your friend look through it as you drop your right hand to your side pocket, concealing the extra coin. Pass the quarter and the stick of gum to your friend as you transfer the tube to your right hand. Drop the tube into your right pocket and with the extra coin that is there. Finally take back the quarter and the gum and put those into another pocket.

4

WITH THINGS YOU WEAR AND CARRY

MONEY BACK GUARANTEE

How it looks:

How do you like my mail order necktie?" you ask, as you display the tie you are wearing by lifting up the ends to show both sides. "I sent away for one of those ten-day trial offers. Wear it for ten days and if I don't like it, I get my money back immediately—no questions asked." You let it be seen that your hands are empty. "Today's the tenth day," you say, fingering the material of the tie as you look down at it, "and I've decided I don't like it."

You fold the end of the tie up against the center and to your apparent surprise two one-dollar bills appear in the fold. "What do you know?" you say, opening out the bills. "There's my money back already. That's one company that really keeps its guarantee."

The secret:

The dollar bills are secretly hidden beneath a safety pin fastened to the back of the tie and are concealed by the way you handle it in showing both sides.

What you need:

A necktie.
Two one-dollar bills, or play money bills.
A medium-sized safety pin, about 1½″ long.

How you fix it:

Tie the necktie as you ordinarily would. Fasten the safety pin *vertically* to the underside of the front part of the tie about halfway down from the top. The pin should go through only one thickness of cloth.

Put the two bills together and fold them horizontally in half from left to right, again from left to right, and then forward from top to bottom. Turn them to bring the left fold to the top and fold them forward once more from top to bottom.

Wedge the folded bills halfway through the bar of the safety pin to hold them securely. Let the tie fall into place against your shirt. You can safely wear the tie that way for as long as necessary before showing the trick and there is little danger that anyone will spot the hidden bills.

What you do:

Let it be seen that your hands are empty without directly calling attention to the fact as you talk about your "mail order necktie." Turn your right hand palm upward and run the fingers of that hand up the underside of the front part of the tie, with your thumb above, until your palm is cupped under the safety-pinned bills.

With your fingers covering the bills, flip the tie up from the front of your shirt so that the bottom tip of the tie goes over your right shoulder. At the same time, with your left hand holding the other end of the tie in the same way, flip that end up so its bottom tip goes to your left shoulder. Hold the tie up to show the undersides of both ends. Then drop the tie into place against your shirt and momentarily take your hands away, again letting it be seen that they are empty.

Now take the front tip of the tie with your left hand and lift it out from your shirt a little as you continue to talk about it. Bring the palm of your right hand up under the center of the tie again so your fingers are beneath the hidden packet of bills and your thumb can press through the cloth from above. Pretend to finger the material critically as you say, "Today's the tenth day, and I've decided I don't like it."

As you finger the material, secretly slide the bills from under the safety pin into the cupped fingers of your right hand, which are covered by the necktie. Close your fingers loosely around the bills. The back of your hand should be up as you lower it to rest on the table. Drop your left hand from the tie and let the tie fall into place once more against your shirt.

Bring your right hand, in which the bills are hidden, back to the center of the tie, *but this time with your fingers at the face of the tie and your thumb underneath.*

Press the hidden bills against the front of the tie. Use your left hand to fold the bottom end of the tie up over your right fingers. Grip the bills through the cloth with your left fingers and immediately remove your right hand. The bills are now inside the fold, which your left hand still holds. Rest your right hand on the table as before.

With your left thumb, squeeze through the material to open out one fold of the bills. Then work your left thumb and fingers to push the bills upward so they slowly emerge from the fold as your fingers gradually allow it to fall open.

Hold the bills that way against the tie and act surprised to see them there. "What do you know?" you say. "There's my money back already." Unfold the bills, drop them separately to the table, and say: "That's one company that really keeps its guarantee."

MUSICAL COMB

How it looks:

"Did you ever play a comb?" you ask, as you reach into your inside jacket pocket for one. "If you wrap tissue paper around it and sort of hum through your teeth against the paper, it makes music that sounds like a cross between a harmonica and a kazoo."

You take out a piece of tissue, wrap it around the comb, and give a demonstration. Then you admit, "I'm not a very good musician, am I? So instead of a *mus*-ician, I'll be a *mag*-ician—and make this comb disappear." You suddenly crush the tissue paper, drop it to the table, and show your empty hands. The comb has vanished.

The secret:

As you wrap it in the tissue an elastic cord attached to the comb secretly pulls it out of sight under your jacket. But you pretend the comb is still inside the tissue until the moment when you show that it has disappeared.

What you need:

A piece of tissue paper about 10″ square.

A pocket comb approximately 5″ long.

Elastic cord or a box of rubber bands, two safety pins, and cloth adhesive tape, preferably the same color as the comb.

How you fix it:

The exact length of the elastic depends on the height of the person using it. Start with an elastic that is about two feet long, then rig it and adjust the length until it works well for you. If you use rubber bands instead of elastic cord, make a chain by looping one through another and knotting them end to end until you have the equivalent of a two-foot elastic cord.

Fasten one end of the elastic cord or chain of rubber bands to the comb by tying it around the last large tooth at the right end of the comb. Push it up that tooth to the top, knot it twice to make sure it will hold, and trim off the end. Wind a small strip of cloth adhesive tape around the last two teeth of the comb to keep the elastic from slipping free.

Fasten the other end of the elastic cord to one of the small safety pins by tying it through the little hole at the bottom of the pin. Then push that pin through the center part of the second safety pin to thread the second one onto the elastic. The elastic should slide freely through the second pin.

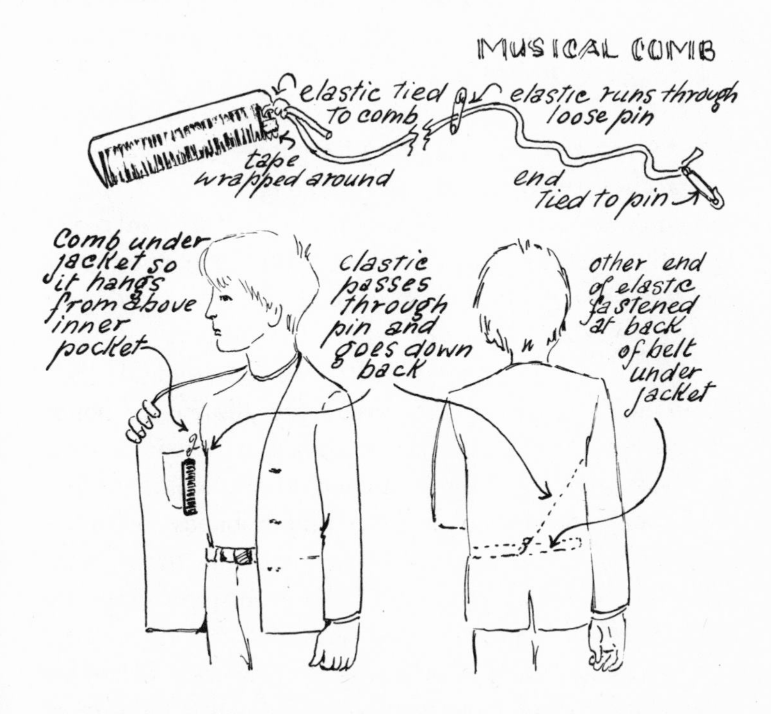

Put your jacket on a table and open it to expose your inner right pocket. Put the comb in that pocket for a moment. Fasten the loose safety pin, with the elastic threaded through it, to your jacket lining just at the inner edge of your pocket, nearest to the armhole of the sleeve.

Now put on your jacket, reach up behind you with both hands, and take the end of the elastic cord. Draw it taut and fasten the safety pin at the end of the elastic to the center of your trousers at the waist, where your jacket will cover it.

It will be necessary to adjust the elastic to the proper tension. To try it, remove the comb from your pocket. Hold your right hand in front of your chest, but a little away from your body, with the palm of your hand toward you. Take the right end of the comb in that hand so your fingers cover the knot and tape. Without changing the position of your hand, release the comb. It should pull through your hand and be drawn under your jacket until it hangs against the safety pin at the edge of your pocket. That is the position the comb will be in when you are ready to show the trick.

Fold the tissue paper in half from left to right, then fold it again from top to bottom. Put the folded paper into your inside jacket pocket. The paper remains folded that way when you use it to wrap up the comb. The comb won't show through the double thickness of paper.

What you do:

Sit at the table so you are leaning forward a little from the waist and your jacket hangs open freely. With your right hand, hold your right lapel to open your jacket slightly. Your left hand reaches in to take the comb. Draw the comb away from the safety pin, until it is at the edge of your jacket. It appears you are taking it from your inner breast pocket. Just as you begin to bring it into view, transfer the comb to your right hand, which is waiting to take it. Your left hand immediately reaches back into your inner pocket and takes out the tissue paper.

Your right hand should hold the comb so your fingers cover the tape and the end tied to the elastic. The hidden elastic runs through your cupped palm and behind your wrist. Display the comb that way as your left hand holds the tissue paper in front of your chest.

Bring your right hand over in front of the paper and place the comb against it. With your left hand, fold the paper forward and down over the comb. As the paper covers it, release the comb. The elastic will pull it through your right hand, which guides it, and draw it back under your jacket. Immediately use your right hand to help fold the paper, and continue to fold it as though the comb were still inside.

Put the folded paper against your lips as if it held the comb and hum against the paper. Pretend to play the "musical comb" and then admit, "I'm not a very good musician. . . . So instead of a *mus*-ician, I'll be a *mag*-ician—and make this comb disappear."

Crush the paper suddenly between your hands and drop it to the table. Show that your hands are empty—the comb has vanished.

THE BUTTON STITCHUATION

How it looks:

After you finish showing some other trick to your friend across the table, you notice that one of the buttons at the front of your shirt is hanging loose. "It's just about to fall off," you say, as you lift it on its hanging thread. "I'd better take it off so it doesn't get lost." You take out a pair of scissors, snip through the thread, and cut the button off your shirt. "I'll wrap it up," you continue, as you bring out a pocket-sized package of facial tissues. Remove one, then say, "I've got a better idea. What's the use of being a magician if you can't do something about things like this?"

Have your friend hold out one hand and place the button on the open palm. Drop the folded tissue on top of it. He can still feel the button in his hand. But when you snap your fingers and lift the tissue away, the button has disappeared. You shake out the tissue to show that the button really has vanished. Crumpling the tissue, you rub it to the spot on your shirt where the button was hanging. As you rub, the button appears again, firmly sewn into place. "It won't come off now," you say, as you rebutton your shirt. "Just as good as new. Sometimes it does help to be a magician."

The secret:

There are really two identical buttons, one hanging by a loose thread outside the buttonhole of your shirt, the other still sewn to your shirt. This button is concealed by the edge of shirting when the shirt is left unbuttoned.

The extra button that you cut loose vanishes from your friend's hand because it is carried away by a tiny pellet of chewing gum on the tissue. When you rub the tissue to the front of your shirt, you get rid of the extra button by dropping it inside your shirtfront. Then you reveal the original button, sewn in place on your shirt where it was from the beginning.

What you need:

A small button to match those on the shirt you intend to wear.

A needle and thread, scissors small enough to fit into your pocket, and chewing gum.

A pocket-sized package of facial tissues.

How you fix it:

Put on the shirt you intend to wear and unbutton the third button from the top. With the needle and thread, make two small holding stitches in the cloth just above that shirt button. Bring the needle out through the buttonhole of the shirt and thread the extra button on the needle. Then bring the needle back through the buttonhole and make another loose stitch or two above the real button on the shirt. Cut off the excess thread, but leave enough so it won't pull loose.

You now have a button hanging loosely in front of the buttonhole, with the outer edge of your shirt covering the real shirt button that lies underneath. The extra button should hang outside the buttonhole by about ¼″ of thread, so it looks as if it were coming loose but is not obvious until you call attention to it.

Chew the gum and put it aside to dry. Take a tiny bit of the dried gum and roll it between your thumb and finger to make a sticky pellet. If you are familiar with the substance known as "magician's wax," you may prefer to use that instead of chewing gum.

Remove a tissue from the pocket-sized packet. Open the tissue, fold it in half from left to right, then in half again from top to bottom, and in half once more from bottom to top. Stick the tiny pellet of gum firmly to the outside center of the folded tissue and put the tissue back into the cellophane wrapper with the others still there. The tissue should be in the same position in the wrapper as it was when you finished refolding it on the table. Keep the pack of tissues in that position and put it into the right pocket of your jacket. Have the scissors in the same pocket.

What you do:

Glance down at your shirtfront, notice the loose button, and call attention to it. Lift it between your finger and thumb, then let it drop so it dangles from the thread. "I'd better take it off so it doesn't get lost," you say. Take the scissors from your pocket, hold the button between your left first finger and thumb, and cut the thread to remove the button. Pull the snipped thread free and put the button and scissors on the table.

Say, "I'll wrap it up," and remove the package of tissues from your pocket. Pull out the top tissue without unfolding it and turn it over as you drop it to the table. The side with the tiny pellet of gum is now face down. Put the packet of tissues back into your pocket. Pretend to change your mind about wrapping up the button and say, "I've got a better idea. What's the use in being a magician if you can't do something about things like this?"

Ask your friend to hold out one hand. Put the button on his palm and leave it there. With your right hand, pick up the folded tissue, thumb underneath and fingers on top. Secretly feel for the pellet of gum with your thumb and lay the folded tissue across your friend's hand so the gum rests squarely on top of the button.

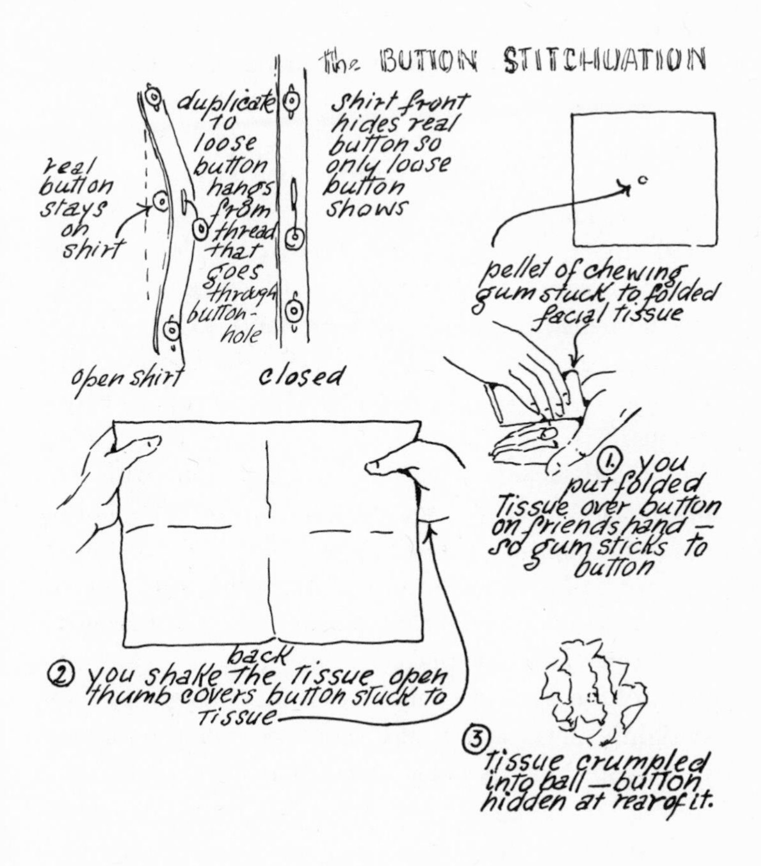

Take your hand away a moment and ask, "Can you still feel the button?" With your right fingertips, press down on the center of the tissue. This not only helps him feel the button but helps you stick the gum firmly *to* the button. Lift your hand off his and ask, "Is the button still there?"

Snap your fingers and say, "But now it has disappeared." As you speak, take the corner of the tissue that is nearest to you between your right first finger and thumb, and lift it off his hand to show that the button has vanished. Gently shake the folded tissue open. Move your right thumb to cover the button, then swing the tissue around to show both sides.

With the help of your left hand, crumple the tissue into a ball, with the hidden button still stuck to the gum. Hold the balled tissue in your right hand. Bring your left hand to the front of your shirt and curl the fingers of that hand inside the opening of your shirt, beneath the empty buttonhole.

Rub the tissue against that part of your shirt with your right hand. As you do, secretly thumb the extra button free of the gum on the balled tissue and let the button fall down inside your shirt. Keep rubbing the tissue to your shirt a moment and then take it away and reveal the button "sewn back into place."

Discard the tissue, test the button by pulling it to show it is tightly sewn, and finally rebutton your shirt as you say, "Sometimes it does help to be a magician."

INCHES AWAY

How it looks:

"Everybody these days seems to be on a diet," you say. "I've been working on a magic formula to make the waistline disappear." Pat your hand to the buckle of your belt at your waist. "No pills, no exercise—eat all the candy, ice cream, and cake you feel like eating. All you have to do with my magic diet is snap your fingers—and your waistline fades away as though you had no waist at all." You snap your fingers and then grasp the buckle of your belt and appear to pull the still-buckled belt right through your body.

"Of course, it's just an illusion," you say, as you unbuckle the belt and put it on the table. "But I do know a sure way to take off a few inches." From your pocket, you take a pair of scissors and a piece of paper that has been made into a tube. Thread the belt through the tube, so it shows at both ends, and bend the tube at the center. With the scissors, you seem to cut right through the paper and belt, cutting both in two. "The trouble is, even with a magic diet—the inches always grow right back again." You pull the belt from the paper and show that it is back in one piece. "I guess there is no way to reduce your beltline permanently," you say, "—except to quit eating."

The secret:

The belt, instead of going around your waist, is doubled upon itself and held in place by the front beltloops of your trousers, with the sides and rear covered by your jacket. The paper tube has a secret slit in it so that when you seem to cut the belt in two you really cut through only the paper.

What you need:

A belt of the length you usually wear. It should be narrow and flexible. When doing the trick you should wear trousers that fit snugly enough to stay up without a belt.

A sturdy pair of pocket-sized scissors that look as if they would cut through thin leather.

An 8½″ × 11″ standard sheet of typing paper and rubber cement or other adhesive.

How you fix it:

Fold the paper in thirds horizontally, as if you were folding a letter to put it into an envelope, with the top fold on the outside. Crease the folds and turn the paper so its open edge is at the bottom. Starting at a point about 2″ from the left, cut a *horizontal* slit across the outer thickness of paper to within 2″ of the right side. Cement the loose edge at the bottom so as to make a flat paper tube.

Now if you hold it so the slit part is against the palm of your left hand, you can squeeze the sides of the tube between the thumb and fingers of that hand to open it up and show the inside. Because of the overlapping inner fold, the slit does not show to anyone looking through the tube from end to end.

To fix the belt so it seems to pull through your waist, first put the belt on a table and buckle it. With the buckle at the front, in the position it would be in if you were wearing it, bring back and front of the belt together, doubled in a flat loop. Take the right end of the looped belt and slide both thicknesses together through the first belt-loop of your trousers on that side. Then slide the left end of the looped belt through the first belt-loop at the left. Straighten it so the buckle is at your waist and tuck the end loops into your trousers at the sides. Put on your jacket to hide the fact that instead of going around your waist the belt really forms a flat semi-circle at the front.

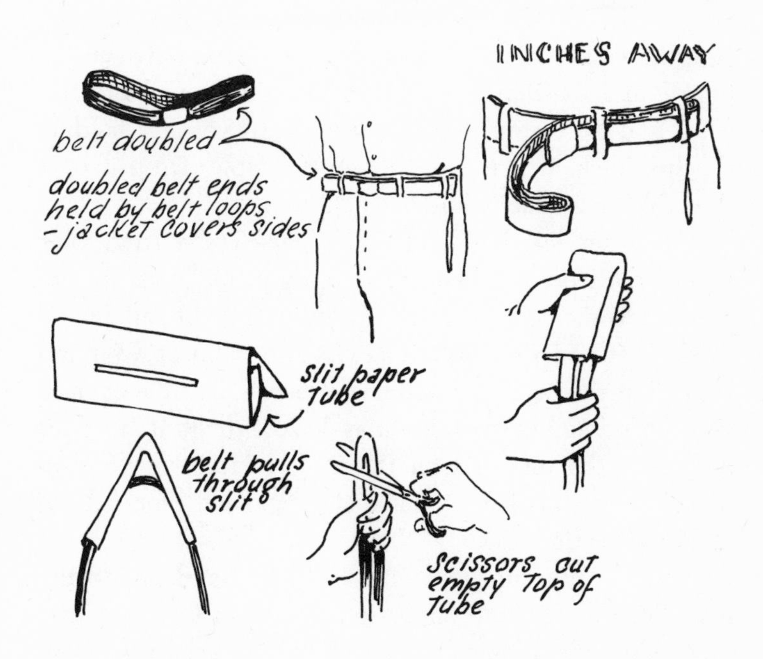

Secretly fixed in advance, the belt may be worn that way for some time, but you can also set it up just before you show the trick by making an excuse to step into another room for a moment. Have the scissors in the right pocket of your jacket and the paper tube, upright with the slit side toward your body, in your inside breast pocket.

What you do:

Pat your waist with your right hand to call attention to the belt without saying anything about it. Then take your hand away as you continue to talk about making your waistline disappear. Grasp the buckle with your right hand and slide the fingers of that hand between the buckle and the rear part of the belt. Pull your hand forward and up in one steady sweep until you are holding the still-buckled belt high above the table. Drop it onto the table, unbuckle it, and leave it there.

With your left hand, take the paper tube from your inner breast pocket, keeping it upright and with the secret slit to the rear. Transfer the tube to your right hand to show it and then rest it across the palm of your left hand. Tilt the far end down and squeeze the tube open so your friend across the table may look through it from his end. Rest the tube flat on the table in front of you, remove the scissors from your pocket, and put them on the table next to the tube.

Hold the tube upright with your left hand, slit to the rear. Put the first two fingers of your right hand into the top of the tube to open it out and pull the back fold away from the rest of it. Take the belt with your right hand and start to feed it down into the top of the tube, so it goes through the rear compartment, next to the slit. Continue to draw it from the table and feed it down through the tube until about half the belt hangs from the bottom end.

Fold the tube towards you, across its center, and let the top end of the belt drop free to the rear. Bring your right hand down a few inches beneath the bottom of the tube and grasp both thicknesses of the belt together in that hand. Pull them down as if straightening them. This secretly pulls the belt through the slit and leaves the folded top of the tube empty. Because of the thickness of the belt it may tear the paper inside the tube a little, but that makes no difference to the performance of the trick.

With your left hand still holding the tube, take the scissors with your right hand. With some show of effort, so it looks as if you are also cutting the belt, cut right across through the center of the folded part of the tube. Drop the scissors, take the end of the belt, and draw it free of the tube to show the belt restored. Crumple the paper tube into your left hand and dispose of it as you put the scissors away in your pocket. Finally feed the belt into the loops around your waist and buckle it normally into place.

RINGING THE KEYS

How it looks:

"Did you ever have trouble trying to find the right key to open a door?" you ask. "I have a key ring that sorts the keys out by itself. They jump around by magic so the key you want is always right where you want it."

From your pocket, you take out a key ring that has two little keys and one big key on it. Hold up your other hand and move the key ring from side to side behind it, demonstrating as you explain, "If you move the key ring to the left, the big key always jumps to the left of the two little keys. If you move it to the right, the big key always jumps to the right of the two little keys. And if you bring it straight up, the big key jumps to the center, between the two little keys."

So far, it is more a joke than a trick, because it is obvious to your friend across the table that you are merely turning the key ring around as you pass it behind your hand. But you are building up the magical surprise that is to come.

"I'll wrap them in my handkerchief," you say, taking a handkerchief from your pocket. "The key ring works just as well in the dark." You wrap up the key ring and pass the wrapped bundle to the left, right, and top of your hand again.

"That should put a big key to the left, a big key to the right, and a big key in the center," you say, as you hand him the handkerchief and invite him to remove the key ring. Instead of two little keys and one big one—he finds three big keys on the ring.

The secret:

There are really two key rings, one of which is concealed in your hand and switched for the other when you take the handkerchief from your pocket. The first part of the trick leads your friend to believe he has guessed the secret, and by the time the real surprise comes the duplicate keys are safely hidden away so there is nothing tricky left for him to discover.

What you need:

Two identical small key rings, about 1″ in diameter, of the plain split-ring type.

Two little keys, such as those supplied with padlocks, and four larger keys, such as car keys. Any old keys of the proper sizes will do.

Two pocket handkerchiefs.

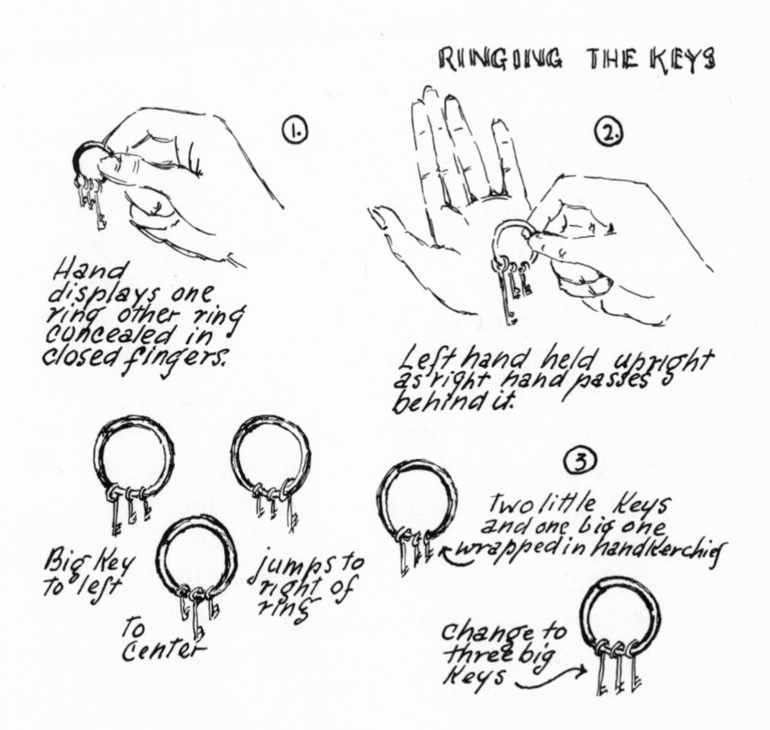

How you fix it:

Put one large key and two small keys on one key ring and put three large keys on the other ring. Unfold one of the handkerchiefs and stuff it into the right pocket of your jacket to serve as a divider, so that the two key rings can be kept in separate parts of the pocket. Put the ring with the one big key and two little keys at the front of that pocket, and the ring with the three large keys at the rear, behind the handkerchief that will keep the two sets apart. Unfold the other handkerchief and put it into the left pocket of your jacket.

What you do:

Reach into the rear of the right pocket with your right hand and get the ring with the three large keys into that hand. Close your second, third and little fingers around them and bring your thumb against your second finger, so that the keys are well concealed. Now reach to the front part of the pocket, take the other ring between your first finger and thumb, and bring that ring out to show it.

Drop the visible key ring onto the table. As you talk about the keys, touch them with the first finger of your right hand to spread them out a little on the ring. Then rest your right hand, which still conceals the other ring, on the table for a moment. Again, pick up the ring from the table between your right first finger and thumb, but grasp it at a point so that the big key hangs on the ring to the right of the two little keys.

Hold your left hand upright in front of you, palm facing you and fingertips toward the ceiling. Say, "If you move the key ring to the left, the big key always jumps to the left of the two little keys." Bring your right hand over behind the palm of your upright left hand, give the key ring a half-turn behind your palm, and continue to move your right hand laterally out to the left. Hold it there to show that the big key is now to the left of the two little ones on the ring.

Now move your right hand across to the right and as it passes behind the palm of your upright left hand give the key ring a half turn and say, "If you move it to the right, the big key always jumps to the right of the little keys." Hold the ring there long enough for your friend to see what has happened. It should be obvious, as you want it to be, that you merely turned the key ring around behind your hand.

Bring your right hand behind the upright palm of your left hand again, and with the help of your left thumb, move one of the small keys right around the ring to put the big key in the center. It makes no difference if what you are doing looks awkward because you want him to think he has caught on to this part of the trick. Lift your right hand straight up above the top of your left hand with the key ring and say, "And if you bring it straight up, the big key jumps to the center, between the two little keys."

Hold the key ring there to let him see the big key at the center of the two small keys. At this point, the second key ring is still hidden in your right hand, as it has been from the start. Lower your left hand so the cupped palm is upwards, and drop the visible key ring from your right first finger and thumb to the palm of your left hand.

Now bring your right hand up and at the same time bring your left hand over on top of it and pretend to transfer the visible key ring from your left hand to your right. But really close your left hand around its keys and let that hand drop to your side. Immediately jingle the other set of keys that have been hidden in your right hand all along. Open your fingers a little to show the keys in that hand without revealing them entirely.

Say, "I'll wrap them in my handkerchief," and reach into your left pocket with your left hand for the handkerchief. *Quietly* put the keys in that hand at the bottom of the pocket and leave them there. Then bring out the handkerchief and shake it open with your left hand.

Bring your right hand up under the handkerchief with its set of keys, grasp them through the cloth with your left hand, and twist the handkerchief around them. Hold your left hand upright as before and move your right hand behind it, first to the left, then to the right, and then to the top, as you say, "That should put a big key to the left, a big key to the right, and a big key in the center."

Put the wrapped keys on the table, let it be seen that your hands are empty, and invite your friend to unwrap the handkerchief and discover for himself that instead of one large key and two little ones there are now three big keys on the key ring.

5

WITH THINGS FROM AROUND THE HOUSE

NAILED

How it looks:

You can tell a lot about people from their nails," you say, holding your hands in front of you and looking down at your fingernails. "It's like palmistry, but instead of reading lines in the hands, you read people's nails. Some are long—some short and blunt. I've made up a couple of little charts."

From your pocket, you remove two small cards and show both sides of each. Penciled on them are rough drawings of different shapes of fingernails, some long, some blunt, some moon-shaped. Point to one design and then another as you continue to display the cards. "This is a surgeon's nail," you say. "And this is a violinist's. This is a baker's nail and this one is a typist's. Over here, this one's a carpenter's nail."

You glance up. "You don't believe me? But it is—a carpenter's nail." As you speak, you bend the cards and a metal nail, the kind that is used to nail wood, suddenly appears. Drop the cards to the table with the metal nail thrust through them, and say, "You see, it *is* a carpenter's nail. You can tell every time."

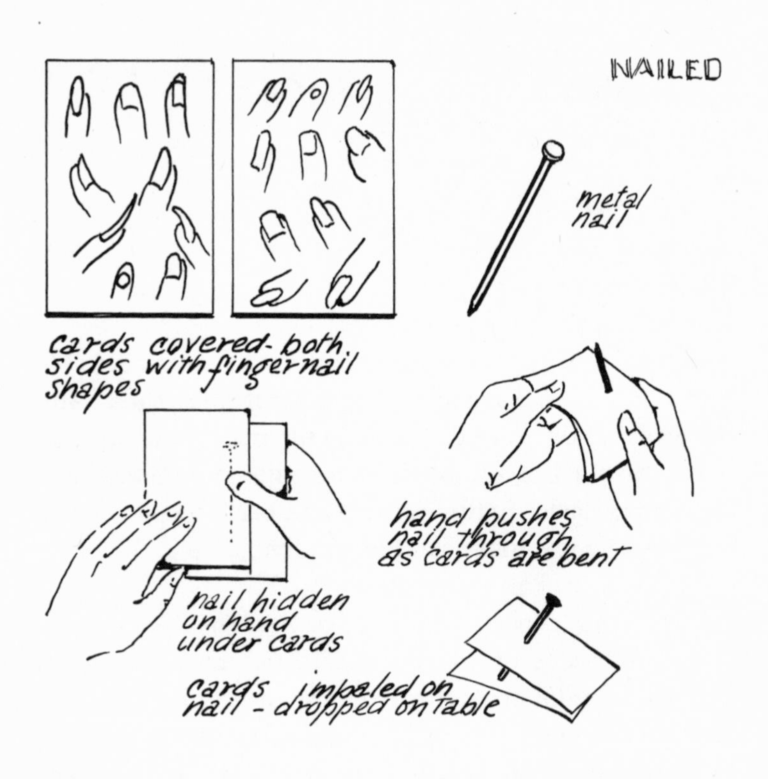

The secret:

The metal nail really is in your hand all the time, but the cards are handled so it seems that you have nothing else. The sudden appearance of the nail comes as both a joke and a surprise. For the proper effect, the whole thing should be presented with mock seriousness.

What you need:

Two blank pieces of thin cardboard, each about the size of a business card.

A metal nail about 1½″ long, with a fairly large head.

A black pencil or marking pen.

How you fix it:

With the pencil or pen, make a number of drawings of various fingernail shapes on both sides of the cards. These need be nothing more than very rough sketches, a few half-circles, a few oblongs, some large, narrow or wide, just enough to suggest the shapes of fingernails. You won't want to spend a lot of time drawing them since the cards are destroyed in showing the trick.

Put the two cards, squared together, lengthwise into the left pocket of your jacket, and rest the metal nail lengthwise in the bottom of the same pocket.

What you do:

It is important throughout this trick that you never deliberately show your hands empty or say that they are; just let it appear they hold nothing but the two cards. Otherwise you would kill the surprise by telegraphing the fact that something else is about to appear.

When you have built up the story to the point where you want to show the cards, reach into your pocket for them with your left hand. Cup the nail so it lies across your fingers. Hold it against the back of the cards, on the side away from your body. Put your thumb on the other side of the cards, nearest to your body. Bring the cards out, held between your thumb and fingers, turn your hand palm upwards, and hold the cards fairly close to the table to show the designs.

At this point, the nail rests lengthwise on your fingers, which are cupped under the two lengthwise cards that cover it. Your thumb is pressed lightly to the center of the top card. Casually let it be seen that your right hand is empty, as you gesture with it and point to the designs that you are talking about on the top card.

With your left thumb, slide the top card forward a little. Take that card between your right thumb and fingers, lift it away and turn it over to show the designs on the other side. Then slide that card back *under* the card that is still on your left hand, so it goes between the card and the nail that lies hidden on your fingers. Immediately take what is now the top card with your right hand, lift it away and show both sides as you talk about the various nail shapes. Put that card back on top of the other one in your left hand.

You are now going to transfer both cards and the hidden nail to the right hand, so that the left hand may be seen empty. To do that, bring your right hand, palm upwards, under your left hand, until the tips of your right fingers touch the knuckles of your left hand from underneath. Now just rest the two cards, with the nail hidden under them, on your right fingers. Withdraw your left hand and press your right thumb lightly to the top of the cards. Your right hand should now be holding the cards in the same position in which they previously were held on your left hand.

Let it be seen that your left hand is empty as you gesture toward the cards on your right hand. With your left hand, remove the top card, show both its sides, and slide it under the card on your right hand, between that card and the hidden nail. Take what is now the top card, show both sides, and put it back on the other one. Point to one of the drawings that you say is the "carpenter's nail."

With your left hand, bend the front ends of both cards together forward and down, as your right fingers thrust the nail through the cards from underneath. Lift the cards away, impaled on the nail, and show the nail going through them. Drop them to the table as you say, "You see, it *is* a carpenter's nail. You can tell every time."

ABSOLUTELY FREE

How it looks:

"Every time you go shopping you get trading stamps to save for valuable free gifts," you say, "so I think it's about time magicians offered free prizes, too." Take an envelope from your pocket and from it remove five yellow-colored trading stamps of a kind popular in your area. Place the stamps in a row on the table. Then you ask your friend across the table to hold out his hand. Count the yellow stamps one at a time into his hand and have him close his fingers over them.

"What would you say if I offered you a brand new washer for only five stamps?" you ask. "That would be a sensational free offer, wouldn't it? I mean, a good washer is worth hundreds of stamps. But there is a catch to it. To get the free washer, you need five . . . *green* stamps. Too bad yours aren't the right kind." You smile. "Don't worry. You've got a magician for a friend." You snap your fingers and have him open his hand. When he does, he discovers that the stamps he has been holding all the while have changed from yellow to green.

You count them out, drop them back into the envelope, and say, "Five green stamps. Just what you need." Then you reach into the envelope. "And here's your free washer." Hand him a small rubber washer, the kind used in bathroom faucets, and say, "Aren't you glad you have a magician for a friend?"

The secret:

The stamps are double-faced, yellow on one side and green on the other, and you place them on his fingers in such a way that when he closes his hand he automatically turns them over. Success depends on your careful control of his hand and the fact that you plant the idea that you are using ordinary stamps by showing another strip with plain gummed backs in the beginning.

What you need:

Five yellow-colored trading stamps and five green-colored of about the same size, plus a strip of three or four additional yellow stamps. Both kinds should be stamps commonly given by stores in your area. They may be of any two contrasting colors. If trading stamps are not given in the area where you live the trick can be done with postage stamps, but you will have to make up a different story to tell.

A plain business envelope, a small new rubber washer,

and a pair of sharp, small-pointed scissors, such as cuticle scissors.

How you fix it:

Take one of the yellow stamps, moisten its gummed back, place it face down, and then moisten the back of one of the green stamps. Stick the two together, back to back, squared so all the edges meet perfectly. Do that

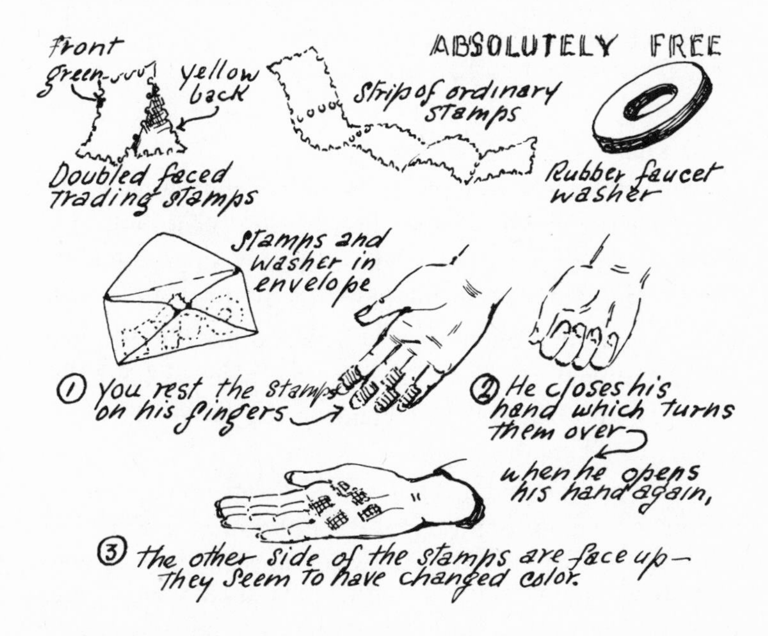

with each set of stamps until you have five that are double-faced, yellow on one side, green on the other. With the small scissors, carefully trim the edges and perforations. Nothing should show that will suggest that the stamps are double-faced.

Stack the five together so that all the yellow faces are in one direction and put them into the envelope with the strip of ordinary stamps and the rubber washer. Have the envelope in the inside breast pocket of your jacket.

What you do:

Take out the envelope and hold it open with the flap up, so your friend across the table can't look down into it but you can. Remove the strip of three yellow stamps, glance at them as if you are considering using them, and turn them so it can be seen that they are ordinary on both sides. Put them aside on the table as you say, "I think I have some separate ones here."

Look into the envelope again and remove each of the faked stamps one at a time, making sure before you take out each stamp that the yellow face is uppermost. Be careful you don't reveal the green backs. Line the stamps in a row on the table in front of you and put the envelope aside. Ask your friend to hold out the palm of his hand. "Just rest the back of your hand on the table," tell him, "so you won't get tired."

With your left hand, lightly hold down the tips of his fingers to keep his hand open. Place the stamps with your right hand, one at a time, on his outstretched fingers, fairly close to the tips of them, as you say, "One, two, three, four, five yellow (use the trade name of them) stamps." Now tell him, "Close your hand," and use your hand to help close his fingers quickly against the palm of his hand. This turns the stamps over inside his hand.

Rest your right hand palm down on top of his closed hand. Keep your hand over his. Ask, "What would you say if I offered you a brand new washer for only five stamps?" Go on with the story until you are ready to let him discover the stamps have changed. Lift your right hand from his, snap your fingers, and ask him to open his hand. As he does, put your left fingers once more on the tips of his to hold his hand open. The yellow stamps have changed to green. With your right finger, spread the stamps on the palm of his hand so he can see all of them, then push them back into a little pile, pick them up, and rest them near your side of the table.

With your right hand, hold the envelope by its flap, so it hangs open. Pick up the stamps with your left hand and count them back into the envelope, one at a time, and say, "Five green stamps. Just what you need." Then reach into the envelope, take out the rubber washer, and say, "And here's your free washer. . . . Aren't you glad you have a magician for a friend?"

RUB-A-CUT

How it looks:

"I was downtown the other day and saw a fellow at a store counter demonstrating a new household gadget. He said it worked like magic, so naturally I bought one," you say. "It's a pair of scissors with an eraser for people who make mistakes." You take out a pair of scissors with an eraser on the points, remove the eraser and put the scissors on the table. "Only $2.98 and the magic is—they really work!"

From your other pocket, you remove a piece of string. "Suppose you have a length of material and you cut it in two," you say, cutting the string with the scissors so that one piece drops to the table. "But then you discover that you've made a mistake—one piece is shorter than the other. All you do is erase where you cut, stretch it a little, and both pieces are the same length."

You stretch the short piece, measure it against the long piece, and they have become the same length. "But suppose you discover that you never should have cut the material at all?" Once more, you rub the eraser to the part that was cut, and hold up the string to show it is all one piece again. "I guess politicians must use scissors like these when they talk about cutting taxes," you say. "They always *talk* about it—but the taxes never seem to get cut."

The secret:

The string is longer than it looks at the start, with part of it secretly doubled up so that you can "stretch" the short piece to the same length as the long one. Its opposite ends have been soaked in rubber cement, so that when you press them together the string seems in one piece again.

What you need:

A four-foot length of soft white string.

An eraser, either the kind that fits on a pencil as a separate cap, or a cube gum eraser.

Sharp-pointed scissors small enough to fit into your jacket pocket.

A felt-tip marking pen.

How you fix it:

Double the string to find the center and mark a dot on

both sides of the string at its center with the pen. Dip the two ends of the string in rubber cement and soak them liberally for a length of about ½″ at each end. Hang the string over the back of a chair to let the ends dry.

At a point about 4″ from one end of the string, start doubling it up in ½″ folds, pleating them tightly against one another as you fold, until you have made about a dozen folds. Then wind some of the string tightly around all the folds three or four times, and with the point of the scissors tuck a small loop of string up under the windings. When you hold the top end of the string, the wound bundle should hang in place and not unravel, but if you pull at the bottom end the windings will come loose.

Loosely gather up the bottom end of the string until you come to the black dot and put that part of the string to the rear of the left pocket of your jacket. Put the other end, with its little bundle of loops, in the front part of the pocket. Close the scissors, firmly impale the eraser on the points so it will stay there, and put the scissors in the right pocket of your jacket.

What you do:

Take out the scissors, remove the eraser from the points, and put scissors and eraser on the table to your right. With your left hand, reach into your other pocket for the string. Inside your pocket, feel for the knot-like little bundle. Grip it between your thumb, on top, and your fingers underneath, and draw the string out of your pocket. Hold the back of your hand toward your friend across the table, with the top end of the string hanging over the top of your hand.

With the little bundle hidden beneath your left thumb, which presses it against your fingers, turn that hand palm outwards for a moment to display the string. Then bring it back with the palm towards you again. Hold the dangling string high above the table and take the scissors with your right hand and cut the string in two at the black dot. The severed piece should fall to the table. Put the scissors aside.

You now have what looks like a short piece of string in your left hand, with your thumb still concealing the part that is bundled. Once more, turn your hand to show both sides and bring the palm back towards you. With your right hand, pick up the long length from the table and hold the two side by side to show the difference in length. Drop the long piece to the table and take the eraser with your right hand. Rub it against the bottom end of the short string and put the eraser aside.

Close your left hand around the bundled part so it is hidden inside your fingers. Pretend to stretch the string, by alternately pulling a little at the top end and then at the bottom with your right hand, until you have pulled it out to its full length. Draw the string through your left hand a few times and then hold it by its very top end, the sticky part, between your left first finger and thumb, so the string dangles down from your hand. With your right hand, pick up the other piece of string from the table by its sticky end, the end without the black dot, and hold the two pieces side by side to show they are now both the same length.

Bring the top end of the right-hand piece against the top end of the left-hand piece, so that your left first finger and thumb hold the two overlapping ends together. Squeeze the two sticky ends together and secretly roll them a little between your thumb and finger so they are firmly and smoothly fastened. To divert attention from what your left hand is doing, speak again of the eraser and reach for it with your right hand. Rub the eraser to the string just beyond the joint held by your left finger and thumb and put the eraser aside.

Take the right end of the string in your right hand, drop the string from your left hand, and hold your right hand high to display the entire length of string in one piece again. Gather it all up into your left hand, drop it into your left pocket, and with your right hand pick up the scissors. Make your final remark about the scissors as if the magic were in the scissors and eraser, not the string.

THE MAGIC BOOKMARK

How it looks:

"When you were reading a book did you ever put it down and lose your place, so you couldn't remember what page you were reading?" you ask, as you take a paperback book from your pocket. "I have just the thing for that. It's a magic bookmark—so you can't ever forget what page you were on."

You take a small bookmark from your pocket and ask your friend to thrust it into the book, between any of the pages, as you riffle them for him. When he has done that, you hand him the closed book with the bookmark in it, and turn your back or turn your head away.

"Now open it to the page where you happened to put the bookmark," you say. "Without reading anything aloud, read the first few lines to yourself. There are several hundred pages in the book. I can't see the page you are reading. But the magic bookmark is telling me that if I had the book I should open it to—page ninety-one. Is that the page you happen to be reading?" When he says it is, you then tell him the words at the top of the page he is reading to himself. "I'm not reading your mind," you say. "It's nothing like that. I'm just listening to what the magic bookmark is telling me."

The secret:

The book is fixed so that when the pages are riffled it always opens to the same page, one whose number and first few sentences you have memorized in advance. Although your friend thinks he might have put the bookmark into the book at any page, you handle it so he inserts it at the one page you know.

What you need:

Any paperback book of about 200 pages.
A small plastic or cardboard dagger-shaped bookmark.
A sharp pair of scissors.

How you fix it:

Open the book to some page near the center, say page 91. With the scissors, neatly trim away slightly less than ⅛th of an inch from the entire right-hand edge of that page. Memorize the first few sentences at the top of the page. Have the book and bookmark in one of the pockets of your jacket.

The MAGIC BOOKMARK

one page cut narrower than the others - book opens there

bookmark thrust into book after thumb has riffled down the pages

What you do:

Before showing the trick, you should practice handling the book to get the "feel" of it. To try it, put it in reading position in front of you on a table at which you are seated. Place the tips of your left fingers at the center of the cover. Put the face of your left thumb at the edge of the pages, with the tip of your thumb touching the table. Now, without lifting the spine of the book from the table, bend the entire book as far to the left as you can, and let the edges of the pages riffle down to the table from under your thumb.

You will find the pages always stop falling at the page that you trimmed narrow. With the book flexed in that position, this happens automatically. But you should practice until you can riffle the pages smoothly and rapidly, as if you are merely helping your friend insert the bookmark where he pleases.

When you show the trick, give the bookmark to your friend across the table and ask him to hold it so he can thrust it into the riffled pages ". . . anywhere, purely by chance." Riffle the pages quickly once or twice to show him. Then as you start to riffle them again, slide the book across the table closer to him, so the trimmed page presents itself as he thrusts the bookmark in.

Close the book with the bookmark in it and turn your head away. Ask him to open the book "to the page you chose." Say, "The magic bookmark is telling me that if I had the book I should open it to page ninety-one. Is that the page you happen to be reading?" When he says that it is, tell him to read a few of the sentences to himself, without saying anything aloud. Pretend you are "listening" to what the magic bookmark is telling you, then tell him what those sentences say.

THOUGHTS IN LIQUID COLOR

How it looks:

"They say that when some people dream their dreams are in black and white, but other people dream in full color," you say. "I've been having fun with a color sensitivity test that I read about in a magazine. Would you like to try it with me?"

You have a small glass of water on the table, or you ask for one. From your pocket, you take seven small cards, and show that on the face of each of them there is a spot of a different color: red, yellow, blue, green, purple, brown, and black. "The idea is to turn them all face down so we can't see what the colors are," you say, "then mix them up and take turns removing the cards one by one until there is just one card left—one color chosen entirely by chance."

By each taking turns, in a way that you explain, six of the cards are eliminated without revealing any of their colors. You point to the one remaining face-down card. "You have no idea which color is on that one," you say, "and neither have I. But each color has its own vibrations."

From your pocket, you remove a small plastic cup. Pour some water from the glass into the cup "to wash it out," and pour the plain water back into the glass again. Once more, you fill the little cup with plain water. "Now, without letting me see what it is, look at the spot of color on that card we happened to choose," you tell your friend. "Think of that color. Fix your eyes on it. Try to project the vibrations with your mind."

As he thinks of the color, you hold the little plastic cup above the glass and pour it out. But instead of plain water, the liquid that pours from the cup is deep red, and it turns all the water in the glass red. "You're good at projecting color vibrations," you tell him. "I never believed anybody could really do that. But you have. The color in your mind obviously must be red."

The secret:

The cards are eliminated in what seems to be an entirely fair way, but the red card is always the last one left on the table. The little "cup" really is the top cap from a household spray can, many of which are manufactured so that the inside of the cap has two sections. In one part of the cap are a few drops of red food coloring. Water may be poured into and out of the center of the cup, but it doesn't mix with the coloring until you pour it into the other part.

What you need:

Seven small cards, such as business cards, blank on one side.

A large coin to be used for drawing circles, a pencil, a box of coloring crayons, and a rubber band.

A bottle of red food coloring, the kind you use to color cake icing.

The plastic cap from a spray can of a type commonly manufactured for various brands of cleaning fluids, air fresheners, deodorants, shaving creams, and other products. Look at the caps of sprays you may have around the house until you find one that has an inner cap built inside the center of the outer one. One part of the cap is manufactured to go over the outer rim of the can and the other part fits over the push-button spraying device. These are not hard to find. It may be of any size, but the larger the better, as long as it will fit into your jacket pocket. This kind of a cap looks like a small plastic cup, with a smaller inner cup at its center.

You will also need a plastic sandwich bag. Use it to carry the cup in your pocket, so there is no chance the red liquid will stain your clothing.

The water you use should be in a transparent glass if possible, not a paper cup, so the color will show. It is much easier to pour from a small shot-glass than from a large tumbler.

How you fix it:

With the coin and pencil, draw a circle on the face of each card and color each circle with a different crayon. Stack the seven cards together, put the rubber band around them, and have them in your jacket pocket.

Put several drops of red food coloring into the *outer* section of the plastic cap, being careful not to spill any into the inner section. Let the food coloring dry, drop the cap into the plastic bag, and put it into your pocket with the cards.

What you do:

Take the cards from your pocket, remove the rubber band, and show that each card has a spot of a different color. Spread them out face-down on the table, but remember where you put the red one. Mentally keep track of the red card as you slide them around on the table, apparently mixing them.

The following method of eliminating the cards will always force the choice of the red one, *but you must always start first* in picking them up, and you must *never put your own hand on the card that you know is red.* Here is how it goes:

You explain that you and your friend will take turns eliminating the cards one by one, until only one is left "entirely by chance." Put your two hands over any two of the face-down cards spread on the table, *but never the red one.* Ask him to touch one of your hands, and then slide that card aside. Now invite him to put his two hands over any two cards, and you touch one of his hands and eliminate that card. Then you cover two and he touches one of your hands, and so on until all the cards have been removed but one. If he happens to put one of his hands over the card you know is the red, you simply touch his other hand. If neither of the cards he covers is the red one, you can touch either of his hands

since it makes no difference which of those two is eliminated. Because you never cover the red card with one of your hands, he has no chance to eliminate the red one, and it is always the card that remains when all the others have been removed.

"Don't look at it yet," you tell him. "You have no idea which color it is and neither have I. But each color has its own vibrations. I have a color sensitivity device in my pocket." Take the sandwich bag from your pocket, remove the plastic cup, and admit with a smile, "It's really just the cap from a spray can, but it serves as a little cup." Casually show it and then say, "I'd better wash it out."

Hold it fairly high and close to you with your left hand. Pick up the glass of water with your right hand and pour a small amount into the center part of the cup, being careful that none of it spills into the outer section where the food coloring is. Then dump the plain water from the cup back into the glass.

Have your friend look at the spot of color on the card without letting you see it. Again, fill the little cup with water from the glass, but this time so that it spills into both sections and fills the whole cup. Now pour the liquid so that it runs red into the glass and colors all the water in the glass as it mixes.

After you finish the trick, remember to place the cup in the plastic bag before you put it into your pocket, so that none of the wet red coloring gets on your clothes.

6

WITH THINGS FROM THE KITCHEN

THE PRETZEL BENDER

How it looks:

I've just been made an honorary member of the P.B.A.," you say. "That's the Pretzel Benders Association. Would you like to see my membership award?" Take out a paper napkin, remove a rubber band from around it, and open it to reveal a pretzel. Inviting your friend to look it over, you warn, "Please handle it very gently. There's nothing quite so brittle as a pretzel. One tiny snap and it will break into pieces. I'd hate to have anything happen to this one."

You take back the pretzel, fold the napkin around it, and have your friend place his fingers on one end of the package. "Just keep it steady so it doesn't move around," you say. "But don't press down hard or it will break." Then you grip the end of the napkin nearest to you and with apparent effort very slowly start to bend it towards him. "Anybody can twist a pretzel while it's still soft dough, before it's baked," you explain. "But you can't be a member of the P.B.A. until you can bend a pretzel after it has been baked stiff."

You continue bending until your end of the wrapped pretzel is upright and seems to have been bent in half. With the same show of effort, you then straighten it flat. Taking the pretzel from the napkin, you show that it is unharmed. "Not a crack in it," you say, as you wrap it again in the napkin and return it to your pocket. "Now I'm all set to go into business—just as soon as I find somebody who wants his pretzels bent."

The secret:

The paper napkin has a hidden slit through the rear fold so that the pretzel remains flat on the table and only the paper of the napkin is bent forward and then back. The slit is concealed so that the napkin seems unprepared and can be shown from all sides when the pretzel has been wrapped in it.

What you need:

A one-ply white paper napkin, in the standard size of 12½″ × 13″.

A thin pretzel, about 2″ by 3″ in size, of the regular three-looped variety. (It is wise to carry a few spares in case the pretzel should break in your pocket.)

A rubber band and a pair of scissors.

How you fix it:

Napkins usually come packaged with each napkin folded in half and then in half again. Use a napkin that is folded that way, exactly as it comes from the package. Put it on a table so its folded edges are at the left side and at the bottom.

First fold it in half from left to right and crease the fold. Then open it as you would the pages of a book and turn past the center to the last fold, the part of the napkin that is against the surface of the table to the right. With the scissors, cut a horizontal slit across the middle of that part of the napkin, through both thicknesses of paper, from the center crease to within ½″ of the right edge.

Now open the napkin again to the center, the way it was when you first took it from the package. Bend down the right top corners of that part as you might bend a book page to mark the place, so the center thicknesses of paper are separated at that corner from those at the rear. Lightly crease the bend.

Put the pretzel vertically at the center part of the napkin, to the right of the middle crease, and close the napkin over it from left to right. Feel through the napkin to find the top edge of the pretzel and fold the napkin forward and under at that point. Then fold the bottom end of the napkin down and under the bottom edge of the pretzel. Put the rubber band vertically around the package and have it in the left pocket of your jacket as you start the trick.

What you do:

Handling it carefully to avoid breaking the pretzel, take out the package, casually show all sides, and rest it on the palm of your left hand, with the folded ends down. Remove the rubber band, open out the top and bottom folds, put the napkin vertically on the table, and open it to the center to reveal the pretzel.

"Please handle it very gently," you tell your friend as you give it to him to examine. "There's nothing quite so brittle. One tiny snap and it will break into pieces."

As you talk, flip the napkin closed and rest it vertically on your left hand again. Take back the pretzel and slide it into the side of the closed napkin, *but so it goes into the rear fold instead of the center.* The turned down corners make it easy to find that part of the napkin without fumbling. Slide the pretzel down so it goes halfway through the secret slit, guided from underneath by the fingers of your left hand.

Now fold the top end of the napkin, and then the bottom end, down and under, so the two folded ends meet underneath. Turn the napkin over to show it is fully wrapped around the pretzel on both sides, and then put it on the table *with the folded ends down.* It should be placed rather close to your side of the table, directly in front of you.

Ask your friend to reach across the table and to put the tips of his fingers on the napkin, so that he can feel the pretzel there. "Just keep it steady so it doesn't move around," you say. "But don't press hard or it will break."

While he keeps his fingers on that end of the wrapped pretzel, bring both your hands, palms down, to the end nearest you. With your fingers in front and your thumbs at the rear, grip the napkin and very slowly work that end upward, bending only the paper as the pretzel secretly extends through the slit that lets it remain flat on the table under cover of the napkin.

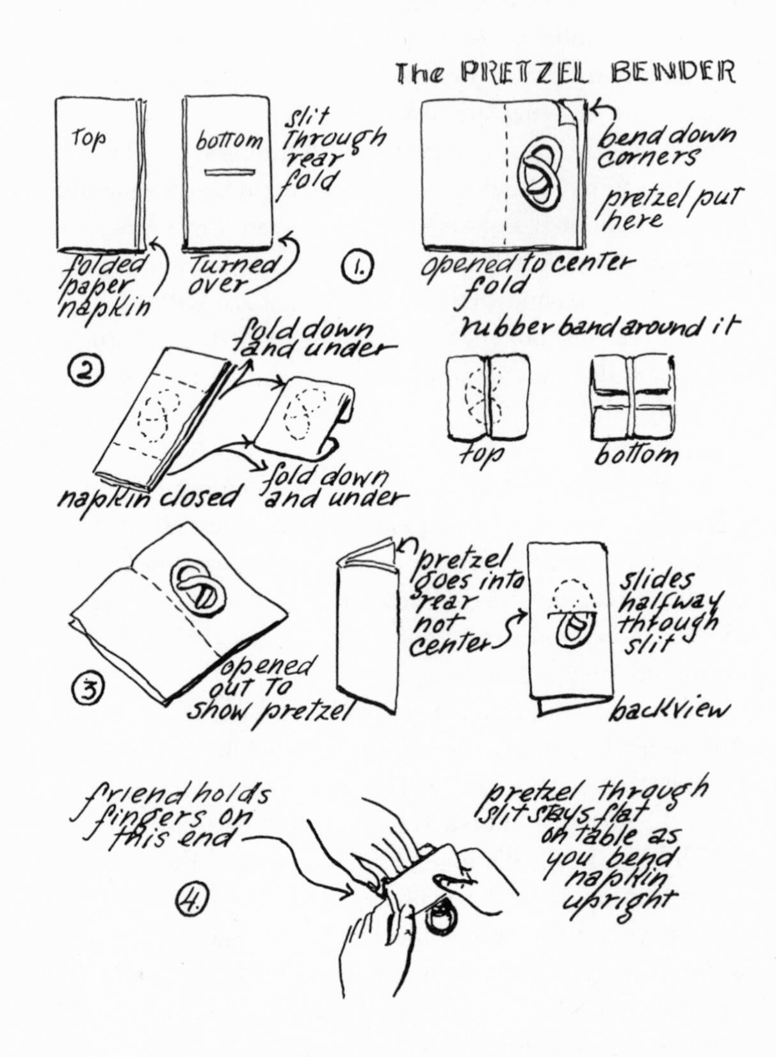
The PRETZEL BENDER
top
bottom
slit through rear fold
folded paper napkin
Turned over
1.
bend down corners
pretzel put here
opened to center fold
2.
fold down and under
napkin closed
fold down and under
rubber band around it
top
bottom
3.
opened out to show pretzel
pretzel goes into rear not center
slides halfway through slit
backview
friend holds fingers on this end
4.
pretzel through slit stays flat on table as you bend napkin upright

Pretending that it takes considerable effort, continue to bend your end of the napkin forward until it is upright at the center. Then, just as slowly, work your end of the napkin down towards you again until it is flat on the table.

Hold your left hand close to the table and put the still folded napkin on it. With your right hand, reach into the side of the napkin and remove the pretzel, display it, and rest it on the table. Open out the two ends of the napkin, then open the napkin to the center. Put the pretzel on it as it was at the start and leave it there a moment so your friend can see that the napkin appears to be untricked in any way.

Finally close the napkin from left to right, fold the ends down and under, snap the rubber band around it, and show both sides as you put it back into your pocket. Say, "Now I'm all set to go into business—just as soon as I find somebody who wants his pretzels bent."

DAYLIGHT ROBBERY

How it looks:

"There is about to be a robbery," you say. "But don't worry, there's no gold to be stolen—only a lump of silver." You take a small container from your pocket, uncap it and dump half a dozen silvery foil-wrapped cubes on the table. "Really they're beef bouillon cubes," you explain, "because I didn't happen to have any lumps of silver around the house. But they look like lumps of silver."

You invite him to look them over and to choose one. "Consider it a treasure that you intend to guard," you tell him. "We'll make some security arrangements." Bringing out a spool, a threaded needle and a pair of scissors, you run the thread through the center of the cube and ask him to hold the ends, so the cube is securely fastened on the thread stretched between his two hands. "I'm sure you'll agree that nobody could steal the silver from you," you say. "Anyhow, not in broad daylight."

But you reach up, pluck the cube from the center of the thread, and drop it to the table. He is left holding the empty thread and when you invite him to examine the cube, he finds nothing about it to explain how you took it from him by pulling it right through the thread. "Solid silver," you say, "except for the hole that we made with the needle."

The secret:

Because of its silver foil wrapping a bouillon cube looks sturdy and solid, an idea that you help to plant by talking about a "lump of silver." But the inside is soft and the foil tears as easily as paper. You really do tear the cube from the thread, under cover of your fingers, and then let a duplicate cube, which was hidden in your hand, fall to the table in place of the torn one. The handling is planned to let you start and finish the trick with both hands empty.

What you need:

A container of silver foil-wrapped bouillon cubes. Various brands come in containers of different sizes. You want one with a fairly wide mouth, not a slender tube. The top opening should be about 2″ in diameter, large enough so you can dump cubes into it without fumbling.

A spool of strong white cotton thread, such as a #8 buttonhole thread, a fairly large needle, and a pair of scissors that will fit into your pocket.

How you fix it:

Put five or six foil-wrapped bouillon cubes into the container and have that in the right pocket of your jacket. Take another of the cubes, run the needle through the center to make a hole, remove the needle, and have that cube in the left pocket of your jacket.

Unwind some of the thread, but leave it attached to the spool. Thread the needle and draw about 4″ of the thread through the eye so it doesn't pull free. Then wind the thread back on the spool and stick the point of the needle down under the thread to hold spool and needle together until you are ready to use them. Put that and the scissors into your left pocket, where you have the cube with the hole through it.

What you do:

Take out the container, uncap it, and dump the cubes on the table. Leave them and the container at one side of the table until the end of the trick. Talk about the "lumps of silver" and invite your friend to choose one and to "consider it a treasure." Speak about the "security arrangements" you intend to make and take the spool and scissors from your other pocket. Pull the needle from the spool, unwind about three feet of thread, cut it at that length, and put the spool and scissors on the table.

Let it be seen that your hands are empty. Take up the needle and run the thread through the center of the cube. Draw the thread through until the cube is at the middle of it. Then put down the threaded cube pull the needle from the end of the thread, and stick the point of the needle under the thread on the spool to hold it as before. Once again, rest the spool on the table.

Pick up the ends of the thread that runs through the cube. Hold one end in each hand, stretch your hands apart, and tilt the thread up and down so that the cube slides back and forth on it. Bring the thread level, so the cube is at its center, and explain to your friend that you want him to hold the thread that way. Give him one end, have him wrap a little of the thread around his fingers, and then give him the other end to hold the same way with his other hand. Have him hold it so the thread is stretched taut.

While you are explaining how you want him to hold it in front of him, pick up the spool and scissors with your left hand and casually put them into your left pocket, as if to clear the table to make more room. With your hand inside your pocket, get the duplicate cube into your fingers. Close your third and little fingers loosely around it and bring your hand out, palm downwards, to rest it on the table a moment.

Now bring that hand over the thread he is holding. Grip the visible cube firmly with your thumb and first two fingers and under the cover of your hand pull the cube down off the thread with one even pull. The thread will cut through the cube and foil as you pluck it free. Immediately let the duplicate cube fall from your fingers to the table and conceal the torn one by closing your fingers around it as you continue to bring your hand on down to rest on the table.

Invite him to examine the cube that has fallen to the table. While he does that, gather up the other cubes with your left hand and drop them into the plastic container, adding the torn one that is still in your hand. Cap the

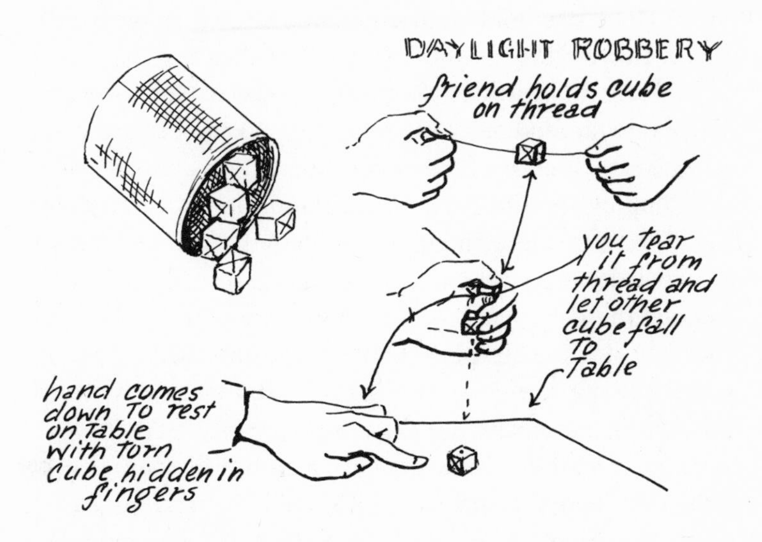

container and put it aside for a moment before you finally return it to your pocket as you finish clearing everything away.

TEA TEASE

How it looks:

You take a small paper bag from your pocket and from the bag remove three cubes of sugar. The bag, as you show, is otherwise empty. "I've marked each of these cubes with my pen so we can play a little word game," you say. "Sugar goes with eating, so I have marked an 'E' on the sides of the first cube, an 'A' on the sides of the second, and a 'T' on the sides of the third. Put them together and they spell 'EAT'."

You put the cubes together on the table and spell the word. "There are only two other words you can spell with these three letters, and strangely enough both those words also have to do with eating," you explain, moving the cubes around as you spell with them. "The second word is 'ate,' and the third word is 'tea'."

Dropping the three cubes back into the paper bag, you say, "The game is a simple one. All you have to remember is which letters I take out." You reach into the bag and remove the cube marked "A," show it to your friend, and then put it into your pocket. Reaching into the bag again, you draw out the cube marked "E", show that, and also put it into your pocket.

"Now which one does that leave in the bag?" you ask. When he answers that the "T" is left, you say, "That's absolutely right. All that's left is the *tea*." You reach in and take out a little bag of tea, hanging by its string from the paper tag. Showing the paper bag empty again, you hand him the tea bag and say, "Here's your tea—I'm sorry I have no sugar left to go with it."

The secret:

The tea bag is concealed in your hand when you first remove the sugar cubes to show them. When you drop them back into the bag, the tea bag goes with them and remains in the paper bag until the end. You secretly steal out the sugar cube marked "T" in handling the others and put it into your pocket with them, so there is nothing left to discover at the end but the unexpected bag of tea.

What you need:

A small paper bag, the kind commonly known as a "candy bag."

Three cubes of sugar without paper wrappings.

A tea bag with its attached string and tag.

A felt-tipped marking pen.

How you fix it:

With the pen, print the letter "E" on all sides of the first cube, "A" on all sides of the second, and "T" on all sides of the third. Trace over the letters to make them as large and as bold as possible. Put the three marked cubes into the paper bag.

Fold the tea bag into a small bundle, wrap its string around it, and bend the paper tag to slide it under the wrapped string so as to hold it all together. Put that into the paper bag with the sugar cubes and have it in the right pocket of your jacket.

What you do:

Take the paper bag from your pocket, rest it on the palm of your left hand, and open out the top of the bag. Tilt the opening toward you so you can see into the bag and reach into it with your right hand. Without hurrying, get the tea bag into the fingers of your right hand and close them around it to hide it; then take the sugar cube marked "E" between your thumb and first finger.

With your lower fingers closed around the tea bag,

bring your hand out palm downwards, and rest the first cube on the table. Look into the bag again and remove each of the other cubes in turn, placing them on the table beside the first one. With your left hand, turn the paper bag upside down and shake it to show it is empty. Put it on the table so the open mouth is toward your friend and he can see for himself that there is nothing inside.

Explain how you have marked the cubes with your pen "so we can play a little word game." Line up the cubes so they spell "EAT," move them around to spell "ATE," and finally to spell "TEA."

Take up the paper bag again and rest it on the palm of your left hand. With your right first finger and thumb, pick up one of the cubes and put it into the bag. At the same time drop the tea bag your fingers have been hiding, leaving it in the bag with the cube. Pick up the second and then the third cubes and put them into the bag.

Tilt the mouth of the bag toward you so you can see into it. Reach in with your right hand, close your fingers around the cube marked "T" to hide it as you previously hid the tea bag. Then take the "E" cube between your first finger and thumb and bring it out. Rest it on the table a moment and point to the letter so your friend clearly sees which one it is. Then pick it up and put it into the right pocket of your jacket, leaving the hidden "T" cube in your pocket with it.

Bring your hand out of your pocket, casually show it empty, and reach into the bag to remove the "A" cube between your finger and thumb. Put that on the table, show which letter it is, then pick it up and put it into your right pocket. Show your hand empty again and put it into the paper bag once more.

While you are asking your friend which one is left, loosen the paper tag of the tea bag from under its string, and grip the tag between your finger and thumb. When he answers that it is the "T," you say, "That's absolutely right. All that's left is the tea."

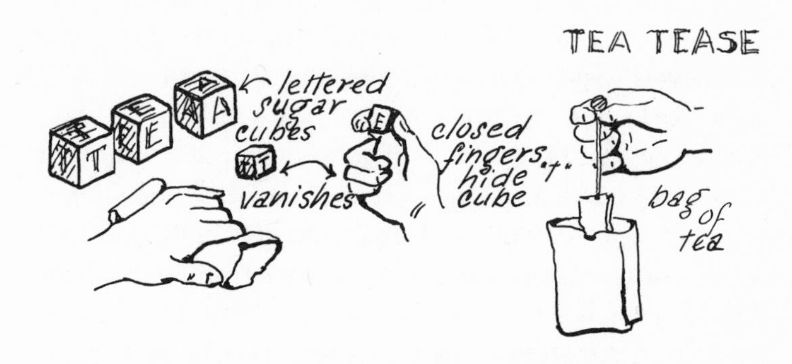

Slowly bring the tea bag out, dangling from its tag, and hand it to him as you say, "Here's your tea." Turn the paper bag upside down, shake it, and put it on the table with its open mouth toward him as you say: "I'm sorry I have no sugar left to go with it."

THREE TIMES SPAGHETTI

How it looks:

"They've got a real special down at the supermarket this week," you say. "Buy one can of beans and you get three cans of spaghetti free." From your pocket, you take out four cards. On three of them are the front labels from cans of spaghetti, and on the fourth a label from a can of baked beans. "Three cans of spaghetti and one of beans," you say, showing them to your friend. "Are you a good shopper? Do you think you can find the beans?"

You mix the labels so that when you spread them out on the table two of the spaghetti labels are face up. You point to each of the others that are face down. "One of those is the can of beans. Which one is it?" you ask. "Pick up the one you think is beans and you'll get the spaghetti free." He picks up one of the two face-down labels, but his guess is wrong—he has chosen the spaghetti.

"I'll make your shopping easier," you tell him. "I'll take one can of spaghetti away." Remove one, put it into your pocket, and mix the three remaining labels face-down. Again he chooses one, and again he gets spaghetti. "I'll make it still easier," you say, removing another of the labels. "That leaves only two. One is the can of beans." He tries again, and once more he gets spaghetti. You put still another label into your pocket, leaving only one face-down label on the table. "This time you should have no trouble," you say. "Pick up the can of beans."

But when he turns the last label over, that also is spaghetti. The beans have vanished. "Would you really like beans?" you ask, tapping the last one against your hand. "Well—here you are." From your hand a shower of dried beans spills out across the table.

The secret:

The card with the baked beans label on it really is double-faced—it has a spaghetti label on its back. You mix them so the faked one is the first one you put away in your pocket, which means that no matter which of the others he chooses he always gets spaghetti. In your pocket you have a handful of dried beans and in putting the third card away you secretly scoop some of them into your fingers to hide until you spill them out on the table at the end.

What you need:

The wrap-around paper labels saved from four cans of spaghetti and one can of baked beans. They should all be about the same size.

A handful of dried beans.

Four unlined 4″ × 6″ office file cards, rubber cement, and a pair of scissors.

How you fix it:

Cut the illustrated face panel from each of the labels and trim all five to a similar size. Cement the four spaghetti labels to the faces of four file cards and trim the cards to the size of the labels. Now cement the baked beans label to the back of one of the spaghetti cards, again trimming the edges. You should now have three spaghetti labels with plain white backs and a fourth that has the face of the baked beans label on its back.

Stack the labels by putting the double-faced card on the table with its spaghetti face up and the other three face-down on top of it. Put all four together into the otherwise empty right pocket of your jacket, with the backs of the cards away from your body. Place the dried beans in the bottom of the same pocket.

What you do:

Reach into your pocket, square up the four cards, and bring them out with a plain back showing. Turn the squared packet of cards face up, so the baked beans label shows on top. Hold them close to the table and deal them out in a horizontal row from right to left. That puts the face-up beans label to your right and three face-up spaghetti labels in a row to the left of it.

Point to them in turn as you explain that you have "three cans of spaghetti and one can of beans." Starting at the left, pick up the labels again, one at a time in the same order, and rest them on the palm of your left hand. Square the four together with the beans label showing on top. Ask your friend, "Are you a good shopper? Do you think you can find this can of beans?"

Turn all four over together, so that they rest face-down on the palm of your left hand. Take what is now the top label, turn it face-up, and show it. Remove it from the top and slide it under all the others so that it is face-up at the bottom of the squared pile. Now take the next one, but *keep that face-down as it is and without turning it over* slide it under all the others. Hold the four close to the table and deal them out in a horizontal row again, from right to left.

The two labels at the ends of the row are face-down and the two labels at the center are face-up. Both that are face-up appear to be spaghetti labels so your friend will assume that one of the two face-down labels at the ends of the row must be the beans. Actually the second label from the right is the double-faced card, with its spaghetti face showing.

Point to the face-down label at the left end of the row and then to the other face-down label at the right and ask, "Which is the can of beans?" Invite your friend to choose one of the two. Whichever one he chooses makes no difference, since they are both spaghetti labels. Turn it face-up and put it on the table out in front of all the others and say, "No. I'm sorry. You got spaghetti."

Tell him, "I'll make your shopping easier. I'll take one can of spaghetti away." Pick up the double-faced spaghetti label that is now at the right end of the row, being careful to hold it so you don't reveal the beans label on the back. Turn your body a little to the left and put that

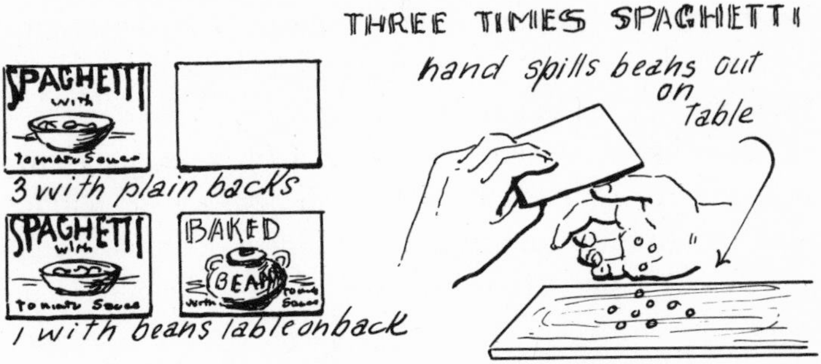

label into the right pocket of your jacket. You have now gotten rid of the faked label. The three that remain on the table are all spaghetti, but one is face-down and your friend assumes that must be the beans.

Turn all three remaining labels face-down, mix them up, and then deal them out in a face-down horizontal row. Ask, "Which of these three is the can of beans?" Invite him to choose one, turn it face-up to show it, and say, "No. I'm sorry. You still got spaghetti."

Take the one he has just chosen and put it away in your pocket. "That leaves only two," you say. "You have a fifty-fifty chance. Which one is beans?" Again he chooses one, and again he gets spaghetti.

Put the one he has chosen into your pocket and as you do, scoop some of the dried beans into your hand and close your fingers around them. Bring your hand out with the beans hidden and rest it on the table. Nod to the one remaining face-down label and say, "This time, even you should have no trouble. Which is the can of beans?"

When he points to the only one left, turn it over with your left hand and show him he is wrong again. It is spaghetti and the beans have vanished. Bring your closed right hand up, concealing the loose beans, and take the label between your right thumb and first finger. Hold it that way a moment as you ask, "Would you really like beans?"

Then take the label with your left hand and tap it against your right hand. As you do, open your hand to spill the beans out on the table.

DATE DUE

OCT 18 '73			
MAR 26 '74			
NOV 12 '74			
FEB 26 '75			
MAR 13 '78			
FEB 11 '92			
OC 1 5 '96			
MY 14 '03			

#22261

√

Severn, Bill

Magic across the table